Messages from the Light

Lorelle Taylor

Peace Angel
Publishing

Copyright © 2022 by Lorelle Taylor
Published by Peace Angel Publishing.

All rights reserved. No part of this book may be reproduced by any mechanical, photographic, or electronic process, or in the form of a phonographic recording, nor may it be stored in a retrieval system, transmitted, or otherwise be copied for public or private use—other than for "fair use" as brief quotations embodied in articles and reviews—without prior written permission of the publisher.

ISBN 978-0-6484786-6-9 Print
ISBN 978-0-6484786-7-6 epub
ISBN 978-0-6484786-8-3 KPF

Contents

Introduction 1
Messages from The Angels and the Higher Self 3
   Introduction from the Angels 3
   Animals' Deaths 4
   Have Fun 8
   A Song –Life Will Be Lovely 10
   Creating in the Past 12
   War is a Reflection of Love 18
   Violence 21
   A Poem –The Light Within 23
   Taking Love to War 24
   The Earth in Transition –Releasing Dark Energy 25
   What Is Love? 29
   Where to Find Peace 29
   Creating Miracles with Love 31
   Teaching Children 33
   Seeing the Light 36
   Life with Shadows 38
   Be a Light unto the World 42
   Express Emotions 44
   Be Peace to Achieve Peace 46
   Focus on the Positives 48
   Follow Your Passion to Enjoyable Sex 50
   Recipe for a Loving World 53

Think Love	55
All Life Is Precious	56
Stewards of the Earth	60
Animals Help the Planet	62
Talking to Animals	63
Working Together Towards the Golden Age	64
Overcoming Negativity	67
Maintaining Positive Energy	69
Confusion About Physical Love	70
Changes on the Planet	72
Helping Bring about the New Age	73
Shining Light on Your Shadows	75
Consider the Consequences to All That Is	77
Time to Shine Your Light	79
Messages from God	**82**
Step out of Your Comfort Zone	82
Moving Forward to a New Earth	90
Life in the New Earth	91
Messages from the Angels	**95**
Influencing Others	95
Removing Shadows	96
Others' Reaction to Your Light	98
Messages from God	**101**
Different Perspectives on Truth	101
Does Evil Exist?	103
The Son of God	105
Fallen Angels	106
The Bible	107
Our Sins	108
The Grand Plan	109
Animal Welfare	111
Crime	113

Sharing Love 114
Procreation 117
You Were Created Perfectly 122
A Different Perspective on Health Issues...................124
What God Is Not 125
God Is Unconditional Love 127
Life 130
War 132
Love Is the Answer...134
The Lion Lies down with the Lamb 136
Which God? 137
Delegation 140

Messages from Archangel Michael 143
Overcoming the Pandemic 143
Moving forward into the New Spirituality................145
Living With COVID 149

Messages from God 153
Masculine Michael...153
Patriarchal Society 155
Gender Change 157
Female Archangels 158
Gender in Relationships..160
Living in a Changing World 161
Helping Animals Help the Planet 166
What Would Love Do Now? 170
Helping The Planet 175
Life in the New Spirituality 180
Understanding Consciousness....................................186
Creating With Love and Faith 193
Violence in Society 197
Be the Change 199
Sex..202

Learning to Love Yourself 205
　　Peace 208
　　Love Lessons 210
　　Visitors from Other Planets 212
　　Changing Form 214
　　The Joy of Service 217
　　Expressing Love 221
　　What is God? 223
　　The Tools for Overcoming Suffering 226
　　The Ego Creates Conflict 230
　　Jesus 233
　　Hate 235
　　Ending Conflict in Palestine/Israel 240
　　Healing after Conflict 243
　　The Lucifer Effect 245
　　Evil Is as Evil Does 247
　　Where We Are Heading 249
　　God's Preferred Name 252

The Lessons 255

Acknowledgements 267

Bibliography 269

"Everything of the light is one. Everything of the light is of God, for God, and for all of God's creation. Everything of the light helps others to be aware of the light, just as Jesus did. It matters not which part of the light these messages come from, for we are all one."

The Angels

Introduction

It had been a few years since I had the urge to have serious conversations with my spiritual helpers and God. Just like Angela in my previous books, *Getting Used to Weird*[1], and *WE ARE ONE*[2], I had to distance myself from God and serious spiritual matters to move forward with my life. My complete focus on spiritual matters at that time had caused an episode of imbalance, which left me feeling vulnerable and afraid. I needed to be more centred in the physical world for a while.

Even though I never stopped conversing with my spiritual team and God, I was learning to trust the truths that came through me, rather than seek truth from any external source.

Then, one day, I began an online shamanism course[3], which recommended starting each day with writing three pages in a journal. The idea is that, when you first wake, your ego mind is still half asleep, allowing your higher self to communicate through you onto these pages.

Once my higher self started writing about serious spiritual matters, it seemed a natural progression to begin formal conversations with my angels and God once more, both early in the morning and during meditations.

There was another hiatus of a couple of years in the middle of the book, while I arranged a move with my husband and dog from Australia to the United Kingdom. Therefore the book encompasses a period of about four years.

Messages from the angels and God appear in *italics*, whereas my commentary and questions to them appear in normal font.

I hope you enjoy these interactions as much as I did, and that you feel inspired to have your own conversations with God and the angels.

You may also be interested in reading some of the blog posts on my website www.lorelletaylor.com, some of which are channelled from the angels or God.

Messages from The Angels and the Higher Self

Introduction from the Angels

Your heart is open when you first awaken. Your heart's focus will always be love.

Love is like a high mountain. It is always there in front of you, obvious and beautiful to behold. It can sometimes look intimidating, but when you start to climb it, you find that it is a gentle slope and an easy grade. You just have to put one foot in front of the other.

The mountains of love are endless. Some are invisible, but there to climb nonetheless. At the peak of each one is a new experience of joy, of ecstasy, with the promise of greater heights ahead. There is nothing to fear in the climb, as there are many travelling companions with you, both visible and invisible. But the mountain of love is alive and helping you along as well. Don't look back and don't look down. Make your own path through the mountains of love, and live in joy and love forever.

❄❄❄

You are the author of your life, just as you are the author of these pages. You have much help with both your life and your pages, but they are your words, your life. You are a child of God, and can create the world and your life into a world and a life that you wish to create, but you cannot do it alone. Your life, like your world, is made up of relationships, and it is your relationships which weave the fabric of your life and of your world. If you put love into your relationships, your life and your world will be beautiful to behold.

Animals' Deaths

(One day, I woke up looking into the eyes of beautiful Cassie, our Doberman.)

I wonder how people who look after a lot of animals and form attachments to them can bear to watch so many of them die, whether by natural causes or otherwise. Even knowing that there is no such thing as death, I would think all of these goodbyes must take their toll. How do you watch so many loved ones die, even when you know that souls choose the time of their deaths?

You know that there is no such thing as death, so why would a number of deaths take their toll?

Because of the lack of the physical body to cuddle, for one. The physical body also keeps your thoughts focused on that being when you're with them, in a way that subtle energy presence may not.

No, Lorelle, but the being can be with you in an instant. Just think of them and they are there.

Ok. I am thinking of Tiddles, our cat from many years ago. I used to feel her loving energy after she passed but not for a long time.

No, Lorelle, she has moved on to other things, but she is available if you really need her.

Need is not the right word. It would be nice to have a pussy cat, and she was a sweet loving cat towards the end.

Yes, she was, Lorelle, after she got over the loss of her mother.

(This was a surprise to me. Tiddles was still a suckling baby when she and her mother appeared in our acreage property. The neighbours didn't know where they had come from any more than we did. When Tiddles was just a few months old, her mother disappeared and we never knew her fate. For her first ten years of life, Tiddles' name was Little Shit, because that was how she acted. For her last ten years, she had a different name, because she had become a loving cat. This was a long time ago, before I had any idea that one could communicate telepathically with other species.)

You don't think she was mourning for ten years, do you?

No, Lorelle, but she did mourn, just as all physical beings do. Even though they, too, understand that, after a physical death, the being is only a thought away, they still miss the physical presence of their loved ones.

Angels, I'm not so happy anymore, because I am remembering all the animals whose babies are stolen from them—all the dairy cows who lose their babies so we can have milk, and all the sheep whose babies are taken to slaughter. All the babies who spend their last hours in a cold, scary place. All the babies who die in pain and fear.

I will share this, Angels, in the hope that others may understand that animals not only feel physical pain but also feel emotional pain. I also hope that readers who already understand this will know their concerns are shared.

Angels, how can we compassionately understand the lion who takes down the baby buffalo, causing pain to another species?

In the wild, there is telepathy between species. You have practised telepathy with other species yourself. These predators only take the ones who are ready to pass.

I don't think their parents would agree.

No, Lorelle. Their parents are like you and know there is no such thing as death, yet still wish to keep their beloved with them in physical form. But there is a soul-to-soul connection between predator and prey, which also used to exist between man and his prey in traditional societies.

Humans have lost the ability to communicate telepathically and the empathy which predator species feel for their prey. They may take a loved one from the herd, but they do it with love—usually. Even in the animal kingdom, there are occasions when thoughts for the individual self overwhelm thoughts for the greater Self, but not often.

Usually, the predator animal is in connection with the All when she takes her prey. This connection with the All, with God, allows her to feel empathy for, not only her chosen prey, but its family as well. This empathy allows her to honour the prey animal even as she offers it to her own family as nourishment.

How many humans even say grace anymore—honouring the food which God has provided for them—let alone honouring the animal and its family members?

Going vegan allows you to know that you are not causing harm to any other sentient being in any conscious way. Of course, you may be causing harm in a number of unconscious ways, and that is a message for another day.

As you have learned, it is best to offer a small prayer of gratitude before you eat, and you might like to tell your readers the prayer you use before each meal (when you don't forget, which is quite often).

"Thank you God for this wonderful meal. Thank you for the plants (and animals) which have given of their fruit and of their lives, so that I may eat. Thank you for the people who have grown them, harvested and picked them, processed them, shipped them, and sold them. And for the person (usually me) who has cooked them."

I usually change the last part these days to: "Thank you for everyone who has contributed to bringing me this meal," because this also takes into account the other animals which help to bring me the meal, such as the bees which pollinated the plants, and the worms which prepared the soil.

❅❅❅

Have Fun

Life is full of responsibilities, but also full of fun. The problem is when we make fun into a responsibility and stop having fun.

We start things in life—from jobs to hobbies—because we think we will enjoy them. But eventually we can begin to think of these activities as things we have to do, and forget our original intention to enjoy ourselves.

It is time now to remember why we are doing what we are doing, and enjoy the process.

Angels, would you like to talk to me this morning?

No, Lorelle. You're doing fine this morning.

I would like some of your profound messages.

I know, but that is the problem. You want to take life too seriously. You want profound messages when sometimes it is not profound messages you need.

Sometimes you need a very light-hearted message. Sometimes you need a joke. Sometimes you need to recapture your joie de vivre.

How?

By doing what you were just doing—by remembering not only why you started that job or that hobby, but remembering why you came into physical form in the first place.

Yes, you all have a life purpose, and sometimes that life purpose can be very serious, but always the main reason for your becoming physical was to have fun—to enjoy life.

How can we recapture our sense of enjoyment?

You are doing it now, Lorelle.

Writing from your heart and from your angels every morning reminds you who you really are. When you remember who you really are, you remember that you are a child of God, and that you have the power within you to not only achieve your life purpose, no matter how serious, but also to enjoy life in the process. There is no point achieving your serious life purpose if you have failed to achieve the main purpose of your life—to enjoy life.

Sometimes it's easier said than done.

Yes, but you know that you can always call on us for help. Whilst it is not our role to tell you jokes, we can if you like.

What did the rabbi say to the priest?

I don't know.

Become the best that you can be, become the person of your dreams, but remember that life is meant to be fun.

Remember that life is like a box of chocolates. There is no point having a box of chocolates and allowing it to sit there and melt. You have to get in and enjoy it, before life becomes a sticky mess. But if it does become a sticky mess, you can still enjoy the chocolates. They are just as tasty in the melted form, as they were before they melted, just a bit more interesting mix of flavours.

You are not very good with the jokes.

I know. Have fun. Have love.

❊❊❊

A Song –Life Will Be Lovely

I woke up writing a song as answer to my prayers for assistance in understanding music better for the choir I was in. I then was able to find an app which helped me to write the music.

Let's take a walk together you and I
Let's make a life together you and I
Let's be in love forever you and I

Chorus:
I will marry you, and you will marry me
Life will be lovely
Love will be the key

Don't be afraid to take a chance
Don't be afraid to find romance
Don't be afraid to be in love
Receive your guidance from above

Chorus

Don't look back now, you've come so far
And when you wish upon a star
Remember God and angels go with you
And there is nothing you can't do

Chorus

We'll make our life together grand
And we won't fail to understand
Love goes with us as we begin
Because it's coming from within

Chorus

And when we grow old and grey
And one of us must go away
We'll know that we can never part

As you are always in my heart

Chorus

❊❊❊

Creating in the Past

I once dreamed that I walked to another area and found a large family of Aboriginal Australians cooking lunch.

The short-haired lady was angry that I was disturbing their lunch, and I asked her if she wanted to come to our New Spirituality Study Group meeting. She said she would come, and I told her I would draw a map but I couldn't remember how to draw a map to get to my house. I told her I would email it, but she said she didn't have email. I said I would bring it back after my husband drew the map for me.

On the way home, it got dark and I had to walk through a person's house where there was a German Shepherd in the yard. I apologised to the dog and he let me pass.

Next, I was at home, unable to remember where the lady lived.

What does this dream mean? At times, I was lucid and aware that there was no way to walk physically from her place to my place.

Any clues, Angels?

No, Lorelle, you'll work it out.

I was so grateful for the song that came through yesterday

I know.

Nothing is coming to me today.

Would you like us to tell you a story?

Yes please.

Once upon a time, there was a lady who lived in a shoe. She had so many children, she didn't know what to do. She cried for help from above, and then she heard that the answer is always love. With love, any problem is surmountable. Every problem disappears with love. You may still face challenges, but problems do not exist when they are looked at with love.

When love is the source of your inspiration, you can do anything you set your mind to. Love will help you climb the highest mountain, sail the most dangerous seas, and walk the hottest desert. There is nowhere you can't go, with love; there is nothing you can't do, with love; there is no one you can't be, with love.

Yesterday morning with love in your heart, you were a song writer. Today with love in your heart, you can be a card reader, or a theoretical physicist like Albert Einstein.

All inspiration comes from love, at least all inspiration for useful things. You can receive inspiration from fear, as well, but it will be inspiration that digs a hole and hides, not inspiration that brings you out in the open to shine your light in the world.

Love will take you places you want to go, including in your dreams.

You wanted to visit a family of Aboriginal Australians in your dreams and ask the lady to your group. She is an image in your mind of someone you would be comfortable having in your group.

But the dream seemed so real.

I know.
Anyway, back to the story.
With love, anything is possible, including creating a woman in your dreams who you can make real.

You mean make seem real?

No, you are a creative being, a creative child of God, and you can create another person on this planet by your dreams and desires.

Well, I don't know what to say to that, except that it is a bit scary. The first thing that comes to mind is: why would I want to create a person, when there are 7 billion people already on this planet?

Because, of those 7 billion people, not one fit the profile that you had been searching for.

I was unaware I had been searching. And why?

You had been searching for someone to join your study group who could help you include people from Indigenous backgrounds, while also helping European Australians understand them. Others didn't fit your profile.

Well, it must have been a ridiculous profile then.

No, Lorelle, just discerning.

Oh, so where is this woman that I have created?

Still in your dreams, Lorelle, but she will manifest in due time, and you will recognise her when you meet her.

When I meet her in person?

Yes.

How does she become manifest in the world?

With the help of a lot of angels.

So she is not born, but created as an adult?

No, Lorelle. She was born in the past. Remember that time is not linear. You can create someone in your present, to be born in your past, to appear in your future.

Wow!

Does this happen all the time?

Yes, Lorelle. Usually you aren't aware of this, as it happens on a higher consciousness level—your higher self is doing the creating, and you, as a physical being, are not made aware of it.

But you know that there have been times in your life when you have felt like you intimately know a complete stranger. These are people you have helped create.

This is making me feel queasy. I don't like the thought of having that much influence on another being.

I know, Lorelle, but it happens all the time. Not just for you, but for everyone. You are creating in the past, the present, and the future in every moment of the now. Each of you is doing that.

Well, I would like to only create in my past, present and future, those beings who will help to achieve the world of my dreams, where peace reigns, love rules, and where every living thing, including Mother Earth, is treated with respect.

I know, Lorelle, and that is what you and countless others have been doing, and this is how you can reach critical mass in such a short time. You just need to work together to do it.

How do we work together, when we create from our higher consciousness? Most of us are unaware of the activity of our higher consciousness. How do we know if it is working with others or not?

It is always working with others, Lorelle, but not always the others that you would prefer, if you were thinking from your authentic self. Your higher consciousness is not always the best, but is always following your wishes both conscious and unconscious. So sometimes you are creating that which you don't want, by your thoughts of that which you don't want.

How can we stop that?

Just by doing that, Lorelle. Only thinking of what you do want, not what you don't want.

Yes, you have to think of what you don't want to see the contrast, but once you decide, only think of what you want.

Sorry, Angels, I am still trying to accept how we create in the past.

Yes, Lorelle. It is a great system that allows you to have what you desire in every moment of the now, providing you have been thinking about what you desire in every moment of your past.

This is too much information to process early in the morning.

I know, Lorelle. Don't worry. You will understand it, and have more questions undoubtedly.

War is a Reflection of Love

What would you like to talk about?

We always talk about love.

Yes, Lorelle, but not today. Today we'll talk about war.

Why war?

Because it seems from your viewpoint that war is the opposite of love, but even war is a reflection of love. Those who make war are generally doing it because they love their country, their tribe, their religion, their people, their family, or themselves. So love is the cause of war as well. What else is caused by love, do you think?

Probably everything.

Yes, Lorelle, love is the cause of everything.
Love bakes cakes; love writes books; love writes songs; love becomes whatever you desire it to be, including peace and love, but love creates its opposite if you so desire as well.
The opposite of love is not hate, but fear. Love for self, family, and country; love for tribe and people creates fear. Sometimes this fear leads to war. Rarely does fear lead to peace.
In order to have peace on your planet, as most of you desire, it is necessary to stop creating fear.

Is that all fears?

No, Lorelle. Some fear is beneficial and does not affect your ability to create peace—fear of heights, for instance.

But most fears are not based on any real danger, but on a lack of love. But even though they show a lack of love, they are caused by love.

It is a hard concept for you to understand—how a lack of something can still be caused by that same something, but it is true. Everything is caused by love.

How can we create love not fear?

In order to create the love end of the spectrum, you have to be the love end of the spectrum. You have to be love.

In truth, everyone is love, and everyone acts from love, but if you want to act from the experience of love and not the lack of love, you have to be love.

Being love is easy. You just need to think love, be love, and act with love. The first step is to think love.

When faced with any fear, including fear of heights, think love. Ask what would love do now?

Angels, wasn't this the recommendation from the book, *Tomorrow's God*[4]?

Yes, Lorelle.

I find it easy to get confused when asking "What would love do now?"

When I'm not meditating, I find that sometimes I get conflicting answers from my active ego mind.

Yes, Lorelle. Your ego loves itself, so it thinks that love would always save itself. That is ok, but if you want to know what unconditional love would do, it is best to ask the question when your ego mind is quiet during meditation, or first thing in the morning.

What would love do now?

Love would write these pages for your book. Love would hurry along and finish all the things you desire and want to achieve this morning, and love would remember to love yourself.

You are a multifaceted being, including your ego self. You need to love all of yourself, including your ego, if you are to manage to love all of other beings, including their egos.

It is easy to love others when your ego voice is quiet, and it is easier when their ego voices are quiet, but if you wish to create a world based on unconditional love, you have to practise loving all of you, and all of them.

You are all magnificent children of God. As God had told you previously, your God-self is that most God-like part of you, and your ego self is that most you-like part of God. But every part of you, every part of each of you, is part of God, and if you desire unconditional love on your planet, you have to unconditionally love all parts of God.

❄❄❄

Violence

Would you like another story?

I'd love another story.

(My husband was talking to our dog beside me, and I asked the angels if I would manage to write with him talking beside me.)

Yes, Lorelle. You're doing fine.

Ok, shoot.

(I was instantly reminded of the lesson I had just had in an online spiritual course about the power of words. I immediately scribbled out the word 'shoot' and replaced it with begin.)

Ok, begin.

Well done. Your words are powerful as you have learned, but so are your thoughts.

If I say or think something before I remember this power, can I take them back somehow?

Not really, Lorelle. You can change your words from shoot to begin as you just did, but the original word is still out there floating around in the vortex, just waiting for more thoughts like it to clump together with it. Once it attracts enough thoughts like it, it can become manifest.

If we are all becoming more enlightened, and using unfortunate words less and less, what will happen to those very old isolated words and thoughts floating around?

Nothing, Lorelle. Once you have created them, they are there forever, but they will not manifest without further thoughts to attach to.

But another spiritual teacher said something about "Cancel. Clear. Delete."

Lorelle, that approach will clear those thoughts from your mind if you have that intention, but it won't erase those thoughts from your vortex.

So it is best not to have thoughts or use words that I don't desire.

As I said before, you can think of what you don't want for a short time, just long enough to see the contrast, but after that think only of what you do want.

What about when we think of things that aren't real like movies and TV programs which contain death and violence? If we turn away for the violent part, and we know that the dead body is really an actor lying on the slab, does it still have an effect?

Not so much, Lorelle, but it really depends on your thoughts and your feelings.

Your thoughts create the thought forms, and your feelings give them weight. If you watch a scary movie, and you are laughing throughout, it would have less of an effect than if you watch a scary movie and are frightened throughout. It's best to avoid all programs containing death and violence, if you can.

Do we perpetuate violence by making films about violence?

Yes, definitely.

Ok, now that I know that I can't watch my favourite TV program anymore, did you want to tell a story?

No, Lorelle, today's conversation has filled your three pages. We will talk again tomorrow.

A Poem –The Light Within

And so it is as I awake
A light comes on inside
A light to guide me through my life
And bring me home alive

I am the joy that I can be
I am the love as well

I am the light unto the world
The light for everyone

Yet, in ev'ry being on the Earth
The light of One God dwells
I merely remind each one of their brilliance
And help to guide them home

❈❈❈

Taking Love to War

And love conquers all, yet we have not yet conquered all of the wars.

No, Lorelle, because people forget to take their love to war.

How can we allow our feminine side to overcome our masculine side, to overcome the masculine need for war?

It is not so much the masculine need for war, Lorelle, but the ego's need. The ego wants to prove it is bigger, better, stronger.
Love is like water. It is soft, yet strong. It is flexible, yet always prevails.

How can we allow our love to override our egos?

By wishing it so. That's all you need do.

I do wish it so.

And so it is.
Manifest your dreams. Your dreams of a world filled with love.
Be love, speak love, and act with love. Love will rule the world.

Thank you, God, for a world filled with love. Thank you for the ability to clean up our mess, and return this beautiful Earth to her pristine state. Thank you for all your gifts. Thank you for a wonderful day. Thank you for love conquering the world.

❄❄❄

The Earth in Transition –Releasing Dark Energy

We are angels, sent to you to tell you secrets of the Earth.
The Earth is going through a transition at the moment. Everyone on the Earth is going through a transition with her.

Is that the animals as well as humans?

The animals are transitioning as well.
As the Earth transitions, she needs to make some adjustments to the way she relates to all her charges. You will find that the weather is changing in different areas. You may find that you feel differently—not sick, but not quite well. You are all attuned to the energy of the Earth, and have to adapt to her changing energy.

There are things that you can do to help her and yourselves, during this time.

As always, you can care for your mother, the Earth, by respecting her, by picking up rubbish, and being careful about what rubbish is deposited in her. You know that, as a species, you create a lot of waste. Mother Earth has a way of recycling natural waste, but you know that some waste is harder for her to recycle, and she needs your help with those things, such as plastic and concrete.

If you can recycle these items yourselves, it will help your mother enormously.

As the Earth transitions, there may be times when you feel sad for no reason, or angry for no reason. There is a fluctuation in the energies, and you, being empathic, feel these feelings along with everyone else.

Just accept these feelings and release them, by doing physical activity, by crying or shouting.

You don't need to analyse these feelings, and you don't need to blame others for them. You certainly don't need to direct them at others as you release them.

Why are these energies increasing now?

To transition with the Earth, each person needs to attain her level of light. To increase your light level, it is necessary to accept and release any darker, heavier energy you carry. This energy may not be yours personally, but as an empath, you feel it nonetheless.

This is why it is not necessary to analyse. You may find

yourself going around in circles, searching for a cause, when, in fact, there may be no immediate cause, but a cause that has developed for generations.

Just accept and release it.

Can we release it back into the Earth, through hugging a tree or gardening and such?

To a certain extent, but some energy will be stickier, and needs processing internally.

Have no fear. This is a positive thing, and is nothing to fear, even though it may seem it at the time.

What about if we don't feel this energy? Some might be worried now that they aren't transitioning if they don't feel this energy.

If you can think love, be love, and act with love in all that you do, you may not experience the effects of the dark energy. You may have accepted and released it, without noticing it.

You can shield yourself from negative energy, but as an empath, if others are feeling it, chances are that you will too. Your animals may not be immune from this energy, for they, too, are empathic beings.

Please have understanding and tolerance for all beings at this time.

May love and peace be with you. Be at peace.

Can I ask: what is the aim of this transition?

The aim is to enlighten the Earth—for everyone to lighten up. This can only occur if the dark, heavy energy already here is accepted and released.

I don't understand. If it is released, is it not then still here?

Once accepted, it is transmuted. As you raise your level of enlightenment, the heavy energy is transmuted into lighter energy, but it first has to be accepted.

Who has to accept it? Anyone on the planet?

Yes. Mother Earth has already transmuted much of this energy, which you have passed to her to transmute. But you can help her at this time by accepting it yourself and releasing it. Once released, it is lighter, and the Earth is able to transition, along with all her charges.

When we do a chakra and aura clearing, we usually send any negative energy to the Earth to transmute. Can we continue to do this?

Yes, this is the best way, but this message is just if you or your fellow beings happen to absorb this energy. You will understand and you don't need to fear, but just accept and release.

Ok. Thank you.

You are welcome. Be at peace.

❋ ❋ ❋

What Is Love?

Never fear. Love is here. Love is all around you. Love is you. Love is all there is. Love is the answer to all questions. And love is the source of all questions.

There is nothing to fear in this world or the next because there is nothing but love here and there.

As you embrace the love that you are, as you embrace the love that surrounds you, you become one with the source of love. You are a child of God. You are one with God and her love. Be at peace.

❋ ❋ ❋

Where to Find Peace

Be the peace you wish to see in the world. You don't need to do anything; just be who you are.

Be the love you wish to see in the world. You don't need to do anything; just be who you are.

You are love; you are peace; you are joy; you are freedom. You came into this world with all of these attributes, and you don't need to do anything special. You just need to be who you are.

Your ego, however, would have you believe that you are none of these things. It tells you that in order to find these things, you have to look outside of yourself. It tells you that you have to do something to find it. Usually the doing involves making someone else do something too.

Some Muslims, who believe that Sharia Law will bring them peace, use war in the vain attempt to achieve peace. Some Western countries declare war on those countries whom they see as the cause of war.

Yet, the war is not to be found externally, and neither is the peace. If you perceive war in the world, the war exists within yourself—between your ego and your true self.

Once you begin to find peace within, you understand that there is no them and us; there is only us; there is only you; there is only "I am".

When God was asked his name, he declared that he would be "I am that I am." I am everyone and everything.

When you go within to find your peace, you find that you are part of "All That Is", part of the great "I am", no greater or lesser than every other person on the planet.

You don't need others to change to your way of life to find peace, love, freedom, healing, and joy. You just need to find the "I am peace; I am love; I am freedom; I am healing" within yourself.

Once you find these within yourself, you know that you are part of the great "I am" and that nothing can destroy your peace, your love, your freedom, or your healing, because that is what you are, eternally.

If there is anything you need to do, it is just to let go of your ego's attachment to fear. It tells you that fear keeps you safe, and when you live from your ego, this is true. But when you live from your true self, you know that there is nothing to fear in this world or the next. You know that you are love, and that love conquers all without war.

You have no more need to declare war on others, than you do on your own ego.

Your ego was a God-given attribute which allows you to experience the world of duality, but you don't need to allow it to rule your life. Use the "I am" part of you to rule your life, and it will always direct you towards peace and love. It will allow you to use your ego as the tool that it was designed to be.

Be at peace; be in love.

You are peace; you are love. You don't need to change anything about yourself. You only need to listen to your true voice, your "I am" voice, and allow your "I am" voice to direct you and to lead your ego voice, not the other way around.

Your ego voice will always keep you in fear of the other, but the other is you. The other is that "I am" part of you—God. Your ego is afraid of God, afraid of that "I am" part of you, because it knows that it is not really needed when you listen to your "I am" voice, so it fears extinction.

Go within and listen to the "I am" voice that dwells there, and you need never fear again.

Creating Miracles with Love

"I am love."
Now that I know that I am love, what can I do?

You can do anything you desire. When you know you are love, and when you act from that "I am love" place within you, there is nothing you cannot do.

When you hear about heroes who have jumped into a pool to save a drowning child when they can't swim themselves, they are acting from love. Or those lifting a heavy car off an injured person, they are acting from love.

Yet, you can bring miracles into everything you do when you act from this place within you. Everything you do becomes a miracle.

In fact, you are miraculous just as you are, because you were created by a miracle of God, and as a miraculous creation of God's, you have the power to create miraculously.

When you settle for the mediocre in your life, it is because you have forgotten who you are.

Now that you know you are love and you have the power to create miracles, there is no stopping you.

Go forth and use your love to create miracles every day. You don't need to risk your life jumping into pools or lifting heavy cars; you just need to focus on love in all that you do, and miracles will flow from you.

You may not recognise them as miracles, but anything done or created with love is a miracle.

What will you create today?

Teaching Children

Lorelle, we are here to tell you a story.

It is about a little girl who grows up to be a woman.

The story starts with the girl being born. She is filled with joy, and is a joy to her parents and the rest of her family.

As she grows, she explores the world around her. She finds some things that are dangerous. She finds the hot water tap and the hard floor when she falls.

Her parents try to protect her from everything dangerous: "Don't touch that." "Don't fall, because it will hurt."

She learns about all the dangers in the world: "Don't talk to strangers." "Don't run, or you might slip." "Don't climb trees, or you might fall."

She soon finds that many of the things she wants to experience are forbidden.

She conforms to the life that her parents have framed for her, outside of which is danger. But as she grows, she becomes more depressed and less joyful. The frame in which she is confined blocks out her joy.

When she is older, she is so used to the frame of her life, she thinks it is normal. She is so accustomed to the depression, she thinks that is what life is.

However, one day she wakes up and sees a world outside the frame. She has the strongest urge to step outside the frame, known as her comfort zone, because she knows that her life purpose lies outside.

Yet, she is frightened. How can she step from the frame and survive, when she has been taught that outside is only danger?

She spends years working up the courage to take baby steps from that frame. In the end, she finds the courage to step outside, then to stride outside, and soon she discovers that outside the frame, there is a life filled with freedom, joy, love, and all the wonderful experiences of life which she has been denying herself.

How might her life have been different, had she grown up without fear? If she had never been confined within a frame? If her frame included everything within the universe? If she was not afraid of any experience?

There are ways to make your children aware of the dangers in life without making them afraid and without confining them within a frame.

We can start by telling our children that there is nothing to fear in this world or the next. All of life can be embraced. All of life can be a joy. Every being on the planet can be looked at with love—from the slithering snake to the large polar bear, from the child in the sandbox with the different coloured skin, to the grown man standing before them in the street.

We can teach our children, not of stranger danger, but of their inner strength. We can teach them that if they ever encounter a situation they are uncomfortable with, they should run away or scream.

We can teach them that they have the means within themselves to know whether any experience is beneficial or not and whether a person is trustworthy or not.

We can help them to develop their inner knowledge, with which they are born. Instead of being told who is to be trusted and who is not by an outside authority, we can teach them they are born with this ability.

When we teach our children to disregard their inner compass and only listen to outside authority, they forget what their inner compass is trying to tell them. It is far better to help them to improve their natural instincts, which are designed to keep them from harm.

But also remember that every soul came into this world to experience certain things in life, and to help others to experience certain things in life. You cannot know what your children's souls have come here to experience.

Maybe they came here to experience precisely those things you have been taught are dangerous.

Perhaps your child wants to grow up to be a mountain climber. How will they ever learn to be that, if they are never allowed to climb anything higher than one foot above the ground?

You can help your child find safe ways to do things, without instilling fear into them. A child can learn to look both ways when crossing the road without being afraid of being run over.

Parents think they are doing the right thing by explaining the dangers, because that is what their parents did. We end up with a planet filled with people afraid to move from their homes, afraid to talk to their neighbours, afraid to live the life they were born to live.

When you tell your child to listen to what their parents and teachers tell them to do and ignore their inner guidance, you end up with a planet filled with depressed people, unable to fulfil their destinies.

The answer is love. The answer is to go within to find your own inner guidance and allow that voice to help you guide your child. Every child is a child of God, with their own internal guidance. You can assist your children to practise relying on their inner guidance as they explore the world.

You can teach them about their spiritual helpers. Their angels and guides are always available, even if they can't see them, although most young children can.

Teach your children to trust their inner guidance, their angels and guides, and the universe, to always keep them safe. But if they ever encounter a situation where they don't feel safe, they can always call on their angels to protect them, and their guides to help them find a solution.

For parents who have been raised in fear, they see fear wherever they look. But your child walking across that high tight rope is walking with angels on either side of her, and a belief that she is unlimited. This is the truth, until you or your society teaches her otherwise.

❉❉❉

Seeing the Light

Love is all there is.

Don't worry if you can't see it outside yourself; you can find it within yourself.

Look to nature and love is obvious. It is not quite so obvious in the world of humans, but it is there nonetheless.

Nature is filled with the light of love, just as it was created. Humans, however, erect a barrier between their light and the outside world, one created by the ego.

Creations of the ego do not reflect the light of love. However, every human, no matter how entrenched in the ego world, is still a creation of the light of love.

When you discover the light of nature, you drop the barrier the ego has created, and your light shines out a little. When you drop the barriers the ego has built to cover your light, your light shines forth for all to see.

Those who see the light in nature, or in other humans whose light shines forth, tend to start noticing their own light, little by little. Soon, their light shines forth as well.

It is possible to allow your light to shine forth for a while, and then to start to create a new barrier, if you become once again ruled by the ego.

The ego doesn't want you to know about the light, because it fears losing control. It knows that, once you begin to live your life in the light, your ego becomes less necessary as your fear of the world diminishes.

Fear of the world, is in fact fear of the light within each being, including yourself. However, once you see the light, "you see the light" in the figurative sense and you realise that there was nothing to fear at all.

There is nothing to fear.

You realise that you are the light, just as everyone else is.

"You are the light of the world. A city built on a hill cannot be hid. No one after lighting a lamp puts it under the bushel basket, but on the lampstand, and it gives light to all in the house. In the same way, let your light shine before others…"

(Matthew 5:14-16)

Jesus reminded people of the light they had within.

Lorelle, you ask whether these messages, and particularly this one, are from your angels or your higher self, but it doesn't matter.

Everything of the light is one. Everything of the light is of God, for God, and for all of God's creation. Everything of the light helps others to be aware of the light, just as Jesus did.

It matters not which part of the light these messages come from, for we are all one.

You are one with the angels, one with God, one with Jesus, one with nature, and one with the rest of humanity.

When you allow your light to be in control of your ego and not the other way around, you can experience this oneness with all of life.

You are the light of the world. Don't hide your light under a bushel basket.

❉ ❉ ❉

Life with Shadows

Peace comes from within. Love comes from within and surrounds you. If you need more love, all you have to do is inhale.

Peace and love are what you are. You are made in the spiritual image and likeness of God—peace and love. Only in the broadest sense are you made in the physical image and likeness of God. Every physical thing is an image of God, and therefore you are too.

You don't have to do anything to be peace and love, except be your true self. There is nothing you need to change, except release the illusions which you have created.

Love is all around you, and you only need breathe it in, but you can breathe it out as well.

To be created in the spiritual image and likeness of God is to be created as a creator. You are able to create and extend your love, just as God has done in creating you. Imagine what you could do, as you extend your love out into the universe. You create a lasting legacy of love for all to witness.

Although you have an ego, it is nothing to be afraid of. Ego is not a dirty word. Your ego was created so that you could live comfortably in the world of duality. It allows you to experience contrasts and shadows in the world and within yourself.

Life is a rich tapestry of feelings and experiences. Without an ego, the tapestry would be rather bland. Your ego allows you to feel the textures of the tapestry. However, appreciating the tapestry doesn't mean that you have to step into it. You can appreciate all of the contours of your life, without allowing the illusions to deflect you from your experience of peace and love.

As you live in this world of here and there, of up and down, it is normal for you to experience shadows within your own being—places where the light has been temporarily hidden from view. There is no need to fear these shadows, only to send them love. With love, your shadows transform into extensions of the light.

Let me give you an example: say that you feel angry at someone one day. You know from your lessons that your anger is just a way for your higher self to let you know that you are thinking in a way that is not in keeping with its wishes. Yet, anger is a natural emotion. When we stuff down our anger because we are afraid of releasing it, it is compounded. Later, it surfaces as rage, which is not a natural emotion.

It is far better to release the anger, acknowledge it as a natural emotion, and to send love to all concerned, including yourself.

Your anger doesn't need to be directed at someone. The real cause of your anger is your feeling of separation from your source, which is only an illusion. You can never be separated from your source of love and light.

The illusion creates the shadow, but your shadow is nothing to fear. Instead, it can be loved.

Your natural emotion of anger allows you to feel the fire inside, which incites action to achieve goals which you may not otherwise have achieved.

In fact, all of your shadows are part of the spectrum of love. If you suppress your shadow side, often it leads to your suppressing the more loving side of that emotion as well. You can close your heart to suppress your shadows and find that you have suppressed your love as well.

It is far better to express emotions as they arise, but in a way which radiates love into the world.

For example, if you are angry at your partner for something he has done, your anger is really an expression of your separation from source.

You can go outside and let out a scream, or punch a pillow, or go for a jog. Flap your wings, just as ducks do after they have a short altercation on the lake. They do this to release their negative energy, and then return to their loving, authentic nature.

Love is the answer to all questions.

When you come back from flapping your wings, if you need more information about how to proceed, just ask what love would do now.

Sometimes the answer is to take action, which will help you alleviate any future anger. If you were a duck, perhaps you might need to fly to a different lake. For you, it might mean to act to address some injustice in the world.

But remember that everyone has free will to change or not. You can point out a need to change with love, but each individual has to decide.

In the meantime, focus on the love which rests within you, and share that love with all concerned.

Love can move mountains. You are love, so you can move mountains, if you believe it so.

Have faith in your ability to be a loving, peaceful child of God. You can always ask God and the angels for help in any of your endeavours.

As you send your love out into the world, you remind others of the love within themselves, and love grows all around you.

Be at peace with all your emotions, and your life will be a peaceful life. You are peace, and you can achieve a peaceful life when you focus on the peace and love within yourself and every being on the planet.

Be at peace.

Be a Light unto the World

Don't be afraid of the dark. The darkness is just a lack of light and there is nothing to fear. If you shine your light on the darkness, it disappears, and there is light once more.

You have sufficient light within yourself to illuminate any situation in which you find yourself, but you may join with others to all shine your light together, wherever you see a lack.

You can always call on us angels and archangels as well. And the Ascended Masters, particularly Jesus, continually add their light to all the world.

So, how do you shine your light in the darkness?

Imagine that you find yourself in a situation that brings fear. The first thing to do is to acknowledge the fear. Next, bless the fear, and thank it for trying to keep you safe. As you bless the fear, you find that your light begins to overcome the darkness. You find your fear begin to diminish. Next, think love continuously to stop the fear from enveloping you. If fear begins to return, merely call on us for help. We will not only keep you safe and offer you guidance to keep you safe, but we will shine our light on the situation as well.

Love conquers all.

You have sufficient love within you to overcome the darkness in any situation, but with our help, and the help of others shining their light, the fear fades and the darkness is overcome.

Go forth confidently into the world, knowing you are a child of God, with the light of God shining within you. Each other person has the same light within, but sometimes we build a wall to separate ourselves from the light within. If someone you encounter has built such a wall, shining your light reminds them of their light within. If a number of you shine your light together on that person, the darkness is overcome.

Each person has free will to choose their wall and remain in the darkness, but when a number of people shine their light on them, it takes much more effort to remain in darkness.

Be a light unto the world. Shine your light into the darkness. It is tempting to remain with others who also shine their lights brightly, but your light is then wasted to a certain extent. When people make a conscious decision, however, to all shine light into the darkness, the darkness fades.

Will you make a conscious decision today, to join with others to spread the light among the darkness?

There are many ways you can do this. The easiest way, is to pray for those who suffer in the darkness, but taking action has more impact. Actions take the force of the light and move it forward.

If you are unsure of where to shine your light, or who to gather with to spread your light, ask during meditation and prayer. The answer will come.

Go forth and share your light with the world. Create a snowball of love which will soon overtake the world. Your large snowballs are sure to cause those walls of darkness to begin to crumble, exposing more and more of the light in those in the darkness.

Express Emotions

Love is all there is, and you are love. But you are capable of a spectrum of emotions that are not strictly love. All of your emotions, from anger to disappointment, to embarrassment allow you to experience life in all its contrasting situations.

When you feel a natural emotion, it is important to express it. As you express these natural emotions, you allow your being to return to an experience of love, joy, and peace—your natural state of being. When you suppress the natural emotions, they simmer below the surface and can stop you from returning to your natural state, until they are expressed in their unnatural state as rage or depression.

Don't be afraid to express your natural emotions through a shout or scream to express anger or crying to express emotional pain. It is far better to be seen expressing these short-lived natural emotions, than to be overwhelmed by unnatural emotions later.

Don't worry if someone witnesses you expressing your natural emotions. I know that you have been taught not to express these emotions in public, and that is understandable because you are all empathic beings, and you can affect others' demeanour with your emotions. Suppressing these emotions can be an act of love for others.

However, it is important for you to include yourself in those you love. If privacy is not possible when you feel a natural emotion, it is far better for you to express it in public, than to suppress it.

Suppressed natural emotions, such as anger, are stored in the body. A body that is overwhelmed with stored emotions can become ill, and many forms of cancer result from suppressed emotions.

You learn to suppress emotions when you are a child, when your parents say "Stop crying or I'll give you something to cry about."

Rather than teaching your children to suppress emotions, teach them to express them in a healthy way. Anger doesn't have to be directed at anyone but can just be expressed in a scream or a shout, in pounding a pillow, or pounding the pavement in a run. Teach children that it is fine to cry when they feel emotional pain.

While children can use their expression of emotions to manipulate their parents, that has more to do with the way parents react to these expressed emotions, and less to do with their expression. All expressed emotions in children should be greeted with love. If you allow your God-self to react to the emotions of others rather than your ego-self, it will always be with love.

In most circumstances, the only reaction necessary is silent presence—allowing the child or other person to know that they don't have to go through the difficulties alone. Love lets them know you are available to help if they need you, but quite often expressing of the emotion is all that is needed for the person to then return to their natural state of being—peace, love, joy.

Be Peace to Achieve Peace

Lorelle, this story is about you.

Me?

No, not you specifically, but you, the human race.

You know, Lorelle, that your race has been praying for miracles to bring peace to your planet. All of you have been praying, but not all have been praying for peace.

Sometimes you don't realise that when you focus on war and violence, you are praying for war and violence. You don't realise that your prayers are being answered.

It is impossible to achieve peace, love, and joy in your experience on your planet, when you focus on the opposite. When you focus on peace, love, and joy, you experience peace, love, and joy.

You are peace, love, and joy. You only need to focus on the peace, love, and joy within you to experience peace, love, and joy. Once you focus on peace, love, and joy, you remove the illusion, the veil which stands between you and your awareness of the truth of who you are.

Don't worry if you can't see it at first. In the stillness, you can find your peace, love, and joy, and if you find it in the stillness of meditation, you are more likely to be able to experience it as you go out into the world. And, if you continue to return to the peace, love, and joy within you, as you go out into the world, you can share it with others.

You are a child of God, and you can create the world that

you desire, but first, you have to recognise who you are—a child of God, made in the spiritual image and likeness of God, as peace, love, and joy. Once you recognise who you are and share that peace, love, and joy with others, you begin to notice that everyone and everything else is made in the image of God as well. Every human on the planet has the potential to be peaceful, loving, and joyful, and sharing your peace, love, and joy with them could be the catalyst they need.

What about those people who are psychopaths or on mind-altering drugs? Do they still have the potential to be all that they were created to be as children of God?

Yes, Lorelle. Psychopaths have certain traits which just need to be understood so they can live in the world, as peace, love, healing, and joy. They have the same potential as anyone else. Those affected by mind-altering drugs always have the potential to stop the drugs and to heal from the effects. God doesn't give up on anyone, and neither need you.

You don't have the omniscience and other attributes to help people like this, but there are some among you who have an affinity with them and who are able to help them achieve their potential.

It doesn't have to take generations to achieve peace on Earth. It just takes faith, love, and a will.

Focus on the Positives

We wanted to talk to you about love. You know it is our favourite topic and yours.

Love is all there is. Love is you and I, you and all of your planet. Love is everything.

Yet you humans have trouble experiencing love. You know that if you think love, you are more likely to experience love, because you attract love towards you. But you are love, so you can experience love all the time, just by being the love that you are.

Most people's thoughts, instead of love, are closer to hate and fear. Instead of attracting love by thinking love or experiencing the love that they are, they experience its opposite.

In the end, even hate and fear are forms of love, because they are usually thought of as a means of loving the self—the little self, as opposed to the big Self, or All That Is. But when you are thinking hateful and fearful thoughts, you attract more hate and more fear.

When you watch violent and fearful events on the news, you attract more violent and fearful events, especially when you watch them repeatedly. Instead you could focus on the positives that always follow violent or scary events, often overlooked by the sensationalising media. A husband shields his wife from gunfire and a man rescues animals in the floods—there are always heroes during frightening events.

There are also heroes in the positive events as well. A child gives her savings to a charity so that others may benefit from her few dollars. An aid worker works tirelessly to help the poor. A nurse works hard every day for little recompense to ensure that someone survives. A teacher takes that little bit longer to prepare the lesson to ensure the children understand the message.

There are many things about every individual human to be celebrated, even those you consider villains. When you see that every human has both positive and negative aspects of their personality, you will understand that there is little that separates you. As Jesus once said: "Let those among you who are without sin cast the first stone."

You may not have murdered someone in this lifetime, but you could have in another lifetime. You may not be a murderer, but you may have had murderous thoughts. "There, but for the grace of God go I," is a saying that you would do well to remember.

Every person on this planet is created in the spiritual likeness of God. Each child of God has the ability to choose in any moment whether they will be love or its opposite. Every person has the ability to choose what is best for the little self, or what is best for the big Self, the All That Is.

When you choose what is best for the big Self, the All That Is, ultimately you are also choosing for the little self as well. However, when you choose what you think is best for the little self, in contrast to choosing for the big Self, you are choosing without all of the facts.

The wise person always chooses for the big Self, because they know that, regardless of appearances, you, too, are part of that big Self, that All That Is.

Your choice for the All That Is is based on love. Your choice for the little self may be based on fear.

When you judge others as better or worse than you, you are choosing in error. When you offer another love, regardless of their appearance, you are giving them the chance to choose love also.

❄❄❄

Follow Your Passion to Enjoyable Sex

Lorelle, today we wanted to talk to you about love again, but this time we wanted to talk about physical love.

You know that you have been reading your book by Tina Louise Spalding about divine sex[5], and we won't cover all of the aspects covered in that book, but we would advise your readers to read that book as well. Just as you got a lot more out of the book than you were expecting, so will others.

Most people have difficulties with physical love, so we believe it is important for us to discuss this with you.

You have learned from Tina's book that the ego is in control of most of what you think is physical love, but you also know there are purer forms which involve all of your energetic body, not just your genitals.

Firstly, we wanted to remind you about the time when you were downloading your first book, and how you learned that vibration is love is healing is joy. So when you share your love, you share your vibration, your healing, and your joy.

This can be done energetically or physically. Because your entire being is involved when you involve your physical and energetic body, giving love which involves both is far more enjoyable for all concerned.

You can share your love with something as simple as the touch of a hand, a hug, or with your whole body when you make passionate love. In Tina's book, she states that without the passion derived from your energetic body, it is difficult to make passionate love. So many people have trouble with this. It is important to first allow passion to the surface. So many people have forgotten how to follow their feelings, and therefore have trouble finding true passion, which can then be shared in love-making.

Your passion can be found in many different areas, but generally, it is not related to physical love-making. Your passion is most aroused when you are creating, and for each of you, your passion is different, because you each have different forms of creation. Once you have learned to follow your feelings and the impulse to create, it is easier to follow your feelings inside the bedroom as well. Start by listening to, and following your feelings in every aspect of your life.

As you know, you have tried to follow your feelings when catching the train, so that you stand in the perfect spot on the platform. Sometimes you are successful and can use the same method for everything you do, or don't do.

You may be sitting at the computer working, for example, and you start to feel uncomfortable. Rather than getting up and moving and finding where your feelings take you, you stay there thinking: "I'll just finish what I'm doing."

Spirit has much more information at its disposal, while your physical conscious self may not always know what's best for you to be doing at the time. Your higher self and spiritual helpers will always steer you in the right direction, but first you have to notice the feelings and then you have to follow them.

As you learned while writing your books, Getting Used to Weird: A Very Different Sort of Love Story *and* WE ARE ONE, *we are happy to give you in-depth lessons in following your feelings. If you ask for those to be only pleasant lessons, you will enjoy them immensely.*

Once you learn to follow your feelings, they will lead to your passion. It might be writing a book, painting a picture, selling real estate, the choices are innumerable. Once you have learned to follow your feelings to your passion during the day, you can also follow your feelings to your passion at night.

If you do not know what passion feels like or how to follow your feelings, ask and we shall help you remember. We can help you find passion in all areas of your life. Allow your heart to open, to feel the feelings you have been taught to believe are wrong.

As children, your feelings led you to discovering your body with pleasure and discovering others' bodies with pleasure. You take delight, as babies, in sucking on your toes and touching your genitals with equal passion.

Soon, you were taught that older children don't suck their toes and don't touch their genitals because it is socially unacceptable. Imagine what the world would be like if all of you adults could retain the flexibility to move your legs into those same positions, and if you could touch your genitals without being thought of as a sex maniac, or nymphomaniac.

You have to live in your society still, so we are not suggesting that you start trying to change its morals by going public with your self-love, but you could achieve a great deal if you allowed yourself a little physical self-love without the guilt which your society has instilled in you.

Why not have a sensual bath, and begin to touch yourself all over, not just your genitals. Do not leave out your genitals, just because someone has taught you that it is wrong. Follow your feelings and ask for our help. We are always available to help you reach greater heights of self-love, and mutual love. Once you have followed your feelings, and touched yourself where it is pleasurable, you are in a much better position to help your lover know what it is that you desire in the bedroom.

Many of you have stopped even giving hugs, so it may take you some time to understand that physical love is just another form of love. It is to be embraced, just as energetic and vibrational love has been embraced by many.

Follow your feelings to physical and energetic bliss. There is nothing to fear if you follow your feelings, because they will only lead you to more physical love and more energetic love.

Don't worry if this all seems new to you to start with. Start small with those things that don't really matter, like what clothes to put on, which elevator to stand in front of, and such.

Recipe for a Loving World

Lorelle, one of the problems with your society is that love is not talked about at all, let alone practised. The love you experience is not what we call love. To really love another, you first must love yourself and have an open heart.

Your society has taught you that it is wrong to love yourself, and it is wrong to love all you meet. If you wish to really bring love into the world, and have a world filled with peace and love, you have to a) talk about love, b) love yourself, and c) open your heart.

Talking about love sounds easy, but most people have trouble talking about all forms of love, from physical love to emotional love, to spiritual love. Learning to talk about love helps you spread it into the world more easily.

As for loving yourself, many people have been told that it is wrong to love yourself physically, even emotionally. You are taught to see it as selfish or self-absorbed if you love yourself, and have forgotten how.

As we discussed previously, a sensual bath, where you can touch all parts of your body with love, is a good place to start physically loving yourself. As for emotional love, recognise all of the ways in which you put yourself down and stop that. Follow your feelings to those things which you are passionate about so you can share your passion with others.

To open your heart, forgive those who have hurt you and have faith that you won't be hurt again. But if you are hurt again, it is necessary to open your heart once more. A heart that has loved and lost is more joyful than a heart that has never loved at all.

As you go out into the world, allow yourself to love all you meet. Your society has taught you that you are only allowed to love your close friends and family. Imagine what the world would be like if you loved everyone and everything. You would soon have the world filled with love and peace you all desire.

For, as you share your love with others, it is naturally returned to you. Love will ripple out into the world in no time, if you follow our recipe:

Talk about love—all forms of love.

Love yourself at every opportunity.

Open your heart to both give and receive love, by first forgiving those who have hurt you.

Think Love

When people forget to think love, they find it difficult to be love and act with love. The ego mind takes over, and the higher consciousness doesn't get a say in the matter.

The ego mind bases all of its decisions and actions on what it learned from early programming from parents and others in your society. Although they were doing the best they could at the time, they based their guidance on their early programming. They based all of their programming on fear.

As you know, fear is just another form of love, in its broadest sense, because fear is designed to keep you safe. But also, as you learned, there is really nothing to fear but fear itself. You are powerful beings who can control your own reality, but you have been raised to believe that you are weak and feeble, and that you need authority figures to keep you safe.

This is not true, unless you believe it so, in which case you create a reality where it is. So how do you get out of this vicious circle?

Love is the answer to this question, as it is the answer to all the rest. With love, anything is possible. You know that we angels are available to help you to achieve your aims. If your aim is think love, be love, and act with love, just ask, and we can help you achieve that, regardless of your programming.

Love can see you climb any mountain and overcome any foe. However, love doesn't necessarily overcome foe in the way you have been taught.

All Life Is Precious

All life is precious, and your life is of no greater value than your foe's. If your aim is to think love, be love, and act with love, then there are no circumstances when you would take another life, even if it means risking your own.

As you know, your life is eternal. Your so-called death is merely a transition from one life to another. Yet all of life is precious, and all life forms on the planet have a life purpose, which may or may not involve giving their lives so that others may live, or so that others may have a valuable spiritual lesson.

You cannot judge another for saving a life, or for taking a life, but you can do all that you can to harm none and preserve life.

God has given all beings a soul purpose, a purpose for their spiritual lives and their physical lives. Even though you learned that you can never take another's life against their will, you know that love would allow others to complete their divine mission in this physical life without judgement.

Can I ask a question now?

Yes, Lorelle.

I understand that punishment is not to be condoned, but what about locking people up to protect the world from them? I know you said that this would be a fear-based decision, but I am thinking of people like psychopaths, who don't seem able to understand how love operates.

Yes, Lorelle, there are some in your society now who have no idea how love operates because of their upbringing, but if you continue to fear such people, you will continue to create a world where they exist.

Love would not fear them, but send them love. Remember that love conquers all.

As you know, conquering doesn't mean prevailing upon another so that they are unable to follow their feelings. Love conquers by allowing all the freedom, peace, and joy that it is.

There is much that you can do to help bring love and peace to the Earth. You can send peace, love, healing, and joy out into the world during your meditation, and this helps enormously. You can call on us for help, and we are happy to serve in any way we can. You can think love often, because thinking love is the first step in being love and acting with love. You can love yourself, and forgive others who have harmed you. You can pray for people to send peace, love, and healing out into the world, and for them to pray for more people doing the same. You can avoid violence in all its forms because it is impossible to think love and violence at the same time. You can share your love with everyone you meet, and hold the intention to act only with love in all that you do.

You know, Lorelle, that one source of pain and suffering on the Earth is the animals that most humans consume. It is true that plants have feelings too, but they are not sentient beings, and food plants have offered themselves as food to feed the world.

However, sentient beings such as pigs, cattle, sheep, and chickens are much more like humans in their desire to stay in their physical lives as long as possible. Although they, too, have offered to come to Earth to be food animals at this time on a spiritual level, on a conscious physical level, their aim is to remain in the physical as long as possible.

Just like humans, animals have soul purposes and life purposes in the physical world, and while it is never possible to take the life of another against their will on a spiritual level, it is certainly possible on a physical level.

I know that there are billions of mouths to feed on your planet now, and you see that as a way to feed them, but it has been proven to you that consuming food animals actually contributes more to starving the people than to feeding them. (…only a fraction of the calories in feed given to livestock make their way into the meat and milk that we consume[6].)

Once people base their decisions on love, both for themselves and for All That Is, they will want to reduce or eliminate their use of animals for food. Freedom, peace, and joy are the natural state of being for all humans and animals, and any person who deprives an animal or human of their freedom, peace, or joy is not acting with love.

Many people would argue that other animals take the lives of animals. Why shouldn't humans?

Yes, Lorelle, and if you want the world to stay in its current state of violence and war, you will continue to use that as an argument to continue what is just a habit for most people.

For some Indigenous people it is still necessary to take the lives of animals in order to survive, and, as Indigenous people are generally closer to their original way of being, they generally take only those animals who are ready to change form.

This is not the case with some Indigenous peoples, nor with nearly all Western peoples. Most people in Western society have no idea where their food comes from.

Many people who are given the task of slaughtering the animals have forgotten their empathy for all sentient beings. Even though they have forgotten it, it still affects them. As they inflict pain and suffering on the food animals, they cause themselves pain and suffering, and those people who consume the meat of these suffering animals are consuming some of that suffering too. They also have forgotten their empathy for both the animals and the slaughterhouse workers who kill their food animals. There is karma involved in both processes.

You correctly mentioned in a blog that you thought that the pain you feel now in empathy for the animals who suffer to bring humans food, is, to a certain extent, a part of that karma. If you were to think love, be love, and act with love, you could not cause pain and suffering to the animals, nor the resulting pain and suffering and karma to the slaughterhouse workers who kill on your behalf.

There is much that you can do to help the situation, Lorelle. You have already learned to be a vegan, and you promote that dietary choice whenever possible, but you know that some people are not ready to make that choice. You can allow them their own freedom, peace, and joy, as they choose the dietary choice that they are willing to have at this time.

Yes, more animals will suffer, but all is well, as one day, all will understand that what they do to other sentient beings, they do to themselves. This is the basis of the empathy that you feel. You feel empathy because you are one with all of life.

❊❊❊

Stewards of the Earth

Lorelle, we were going to talk about the fact that humans have much more control over the turn of events than animals, because they have been given a greater gift of creativity. This great gift was to be used in their intended role as stewards of the Earth, ensuring that Mother Earth and her charges are aided to live in peace, freedom, and joy. However, most humans do not even know this was to be their role. Many humans are only looking out for themselves.

In a world where the focus is more on the little self, those less fortunate are not in a good position to be stewards of the Earth as their attention focuses on survival. Those more fortunate are called to help those less fortunate and also be stewards of the Earth—to ensure that the focus of their lives and of their thoughts is upon All That Is. In helping those less fortunate, they are allowing them to become stewards of the Earth as well.

To do this, those in more fortunate societies need to follow your feelings, because your feelings come from your higher self, and your higher self knows the best course of action in any situation, and who you should be helping, as opposed to those who wish to look after themselves. If you are unsure, please ask us for help, and we will provide you with signs to help guide you towards appropriate action. Your prayers and loving thoughts towards All That Is are immensely powerful also. Because you are such creative beings, when you believe in the power of your thoughts and prayers particularly, you can, indeed, move mountains, as the Bible has told you. Actually moving mountains might not be in the best interests of All That Is, but that hasn't stopped you humans from digging into the Earth and removing vast quantities of mountain, plain, or hill.

The time is now, in the evolution of humans and your planet, for you to work together with other humans, other beings, and the planet herself, to ensure that any future actions are always beneficial, or at the very least, neutral in the impact on others. Don't worry too much about it, though, because worry creates the opposite of what you desire. Instead, hold positive thoughts regarding the future of your planet.

You don't need to know how the current problems will be resolved. When you start to think about the how, worry takes hold because you don't have sufficient information to act. Instead, meditate on the future that you would like to see, where every living thing, and Mother Earth herself, are treated with respect, and are allowed freedom, peace, and joy.

❋❋❋

Animals Help the Planet

Animals, for the most part, are here on the Earth to provide a balancing effect for all the negativity that humans attract. Without the animals, apart from the problems with the physical world, there would also be an energetic problem on the Earth, because the negative energy on the Earth would definitely outweigh the positive.

The trees and animals provide a balancing effect, but humans disrupt this balance, not only with negative energy, but also with actions. Humans chop down trees and drive animals to extinction. As species become extinct, other animals are affected due to the interdependence of all of life. Great damage is being done to entire ecosystems, and to the biosphere as a whole.

The factory farming of food animals also impacts the Earth's energy negatively. Whereas food animals may expect, on a spiritual level, to become food, they do expect a life worth living. Instead of balancing the Earth with positive energy, they too, contribute to the negative energy on the planet. Even though animals are generally more loving than humans, the effect of humans on factory-farmed animals causes them to have negative rather than positive thoughts, thus adding to the negative energy on the planet.

Humans cannot continue to feed their populations in the manner that they have been and allow themselves and the planet to survive. Apart from the effects of food animals on the ecosystems and the biosphere as a whole, the negative energy caused by factory farming is enough to cause grave damage to your planet's ability to sustain itself. Something has to change and change quickly if you are to survive.

We are not trying to frighten you, but merely to point out the facts, in the hope that you will change your ways. Ask us, and we can help you to change your desires for meat and other animal products, and we can help you move towards a meat-free or vegan diet.

❄❄❄

Talking to Animals

We were discussing love in all its forms, animals and the contributions they make. Now we can explore communication with them.

You can communicate telepathically with animals, just as you do with us. You can communicate with them more easily after a brief meditation, when the ego mind is quiet. If you are out walking and wish to communicate with an animal, you can always make an animal's acquaintance on a walk, and then talk to them later, after you have meditated, just as you did with the fairy, Patarina. This will improve your confidence in your abilities, rather than trying and failing to maintain a conversation while out walking.

❄❄❄

Working Together Towards the Golden Age

It was good that you were reminded of your lessons from the book Ask Your Angels[7]. *This is a positive step forward—for you, to revise this information, but also for your readers, to introduce them to the idea of having their own conversations with angels.*

As you learned from the book, there are changes happening both in the physical world that you inhabit, and in the spiritual world where angels live. Love is becoming more prominent on Earth, and it is rearranging the spiritual world. We angels use the love that we are to arrange a different way of being and we are changing our relationship with humans on Earth.

As you read recently, other beings and other humans who reside elsewhere, already have close relationships with their angels. Earthly humans are now becoming more like the rest of physical creation. When you are in regular contact with the angels, you are much happier.

Yes, and even reading about them seems to make me happy.

Yes, you are wired to find joy in the communication we provide, both directly to yourself, and to your fellow humans. You are all one, as you know. So, when you read about a human-angel relationship, it reminds you of your own.

You are a joy to work with, every single one of you. But it is easier to work with you if you know of our existence. Raising your vibration also assists us, as it means we have less work to do, in order for you to hear our communication.

We communicate via your brain, not your ears. But the part of your brain that is affected is near the area of the brain that carries information from your ears. Sometimes people hear us, as if they are hearing the words spoken by a physical person. Sometimes, as in your communications, you just hear a thought, which is translated into words by your brain.

It is a marvellous invention—your brain. You know that your scientists have shown that there is quite a lot of your brain that is unused by your normal daily life. Meditation and spiritual communication use more parts of your brain, but there are still more available, once your species is ready.

We are ready and waiting to help you all move forward into The Golden Age, as it has been called. We need to work together—not only humans and angels, but also the planet and all of its inhabitants, including nature spirits and all the other forms of spiritual helpers, who currently aid those beings on Earth.

Humans can only work in conjunction with the others when they are awake and aware of our presence, but also, only when they attain a certain level of understanding of spiritual matters and let go of some of the heavier energy currently weighing down the planet.

It takes a certain amount of commitment on the part of all concerned. Please work with us to help your fellow humans wake up, and become more enlightened.

In this context, enlightenment just means allowing the light that already exists within each and every one of you to shine brilliantly out into the world. This aids others to awaken, to follow their spiritual paths, and to become part of the solution to the problems facing your planet, rather than the cause.

The angels and other spiritual beings assisting your planet at this time, all have the will to help humans to evolve, and to help the planet move towards its Golden Age. You each can do your part.

The first step *is to think love, be love, and act with love in all that you do. This takes will-power and practice. As you practise being love, you become better at it.*

The second step *is to release all those unloving parts of your behaviour as they arise, which they will, if you focus on love. There is no point feeling guilty about doing something unloving. When you think, say, or do something unloving, either you will recognise it as such, so that you can understand its cause, or we will point it out to you, perhaps via another human. Most unloving behaviours are caused by habits from your earlier programming. Once you recognise these habits, it is possible to change them. But do have patience with yourself. These habits were not created nor released overnight but with awareness, soon they will become a thing of the past.*

*For **the third step**, aim to stay in the present moment, where joy resides. It is impossible to be unhappy if you reside in the present moment, unless you are being tortured, or some drastic action is being taken against you. Even if you have pain, with the love that you are and within the present moment, it is possible to blank out pain, but this takes practice. Start with living in the present moment when life is joyful, or neutral. After you have practised returning to the present moment in easier circumstances, it will be much easier when things get difficult.*

With so many changes happening in the world in order to

bring about the new age, it may be necessary to endure some difficulties. But difficulties are only difficulties if you perceive them as such. If you perceive them as steppingstones to joy and bliss, they are easier to endure.

Regardless of the circumstances you face, your angels are right there with you, helping you as best they can. We must respect your free will so if you need help with a particular project, it is best to ask for help with this specifically.

❈❈❈

Overcoming Negativity

Now, Lorelle, we have talked about many things, but they have all really been about love. The reason for that is clear: everything is love. You are love; I am love; God is love; your best friend is love, as is your worst enemy. We are all made of love. Unfortunately, some people wear a heavy covering over their love, so you have trouble seeing the love within.

Love is light, and in order to share your love with the world, it is necessary to remove the heavy covering that you are wearing, so that your light can be seen. The heavy covering is created by years, lifetimes, and generations of negativity. As you share positivity, you help to reduce the negativity creating these heavy coverings.

When people try to act positively in the face of dire circumstances, others may tell them to behave differently, that they are deluding themselves by trying to be positive. In fact, the opposite is true. You are deluding yourself by even thinking that any situation could ever really have a negative impact upon you, unless you believe it is possible. Since your thoughts and beliefs create your reality, maintaining a positive outlook maintains a positive reality.

However, so many people extend their negativity out into the world that it becomes difficult for positive people to avoid contamination. This is one reason that it is important to surround yourself in white light, and to clear your energy field regularly.

If you send out love into the world, no negativity can adhere to you. This is the same as creating a protective white light energy field around yourself. However, even for those very enlightened people, it is impossible to send love out into the world continuously, so protection and clearing of your energy field are good habits for everyone.

When you create a bubble of white light around yourself, you don't allow negative energy to attach to you. But if you have forgotten to do it, you may have some negative energy in your energy field, and it is important to clear it regularly to ensure that it doesn't build up and cause your light to be covered. Once it builds up into a heavy layer, it is harder to shift, requiring something like an Epsom salts bath and aid from your spiritual helpers to remove it.

But, as with all things, intention is important. You are a powerful, creative, child of God, and if you have the intention to maintain a positive energy field, and to maintain a protective layer around that positive energy field, you can achieve that. There are many meditations designed to protect and clear your energy fields, and you can always ask us angels for help.

❆❆❆

Maintaining Positive Energy

Hello Angels, would you like to talk to me?

Not really, Lorelle, but we will. Just kidding.

Not funny.

I know. This is the way that humans act, but angels do not act in an unloving way—ever. This is how you can recognise that the messages are coming from us. Never carry on a conversation with an entity which makes you feel uncomfortable, and leaves you feeling anything other than joy.

We are filled with love and joy, and we like to share it if we can, to as many humans as we can. That is another reason why we want humans to communicate with us.

You are right in what you were thinking that all beings are made of love and joy, but, even in the spiritual arena, there are entities who have shrouded their light and love in darkness. This is another reason to protect yourself, and to ask only for communication from angels and high-vibrational guides. That way, you are less likely to attract the attention of negative entities.

Keeping your thoughts focused on love also helps, as does sending love out into the world. If you send your love out to all entities shrouded in darkness, you help to lift the shrouds from their light, and allow the light to shine through. This applies mostly to humans, but also to some negative entities on the spiritual side as well.

Confusion About Physical Love

As you remember from our previous discussions, sex and love are one and the same. It is impossible to have sex without love, even though it is possible not to experience that love, in the case of rape and prostitution. However, it is still an act of love.

Humans have been taught that some forms of love are allowed, while others are not, thus creating confusion. As all humans are born with an innate sense of right and wrong learned from their higher selves, they are born wanting to love themselves and all others equally. They want to share their love in any way possible. However, once they are born into a human society, they are taught the laws of the society which dictate how and whom they can love: a contradiction between their natural behaviour and the behaviour they are told is acceptable. Often this leads to great difficulties.

Sometimes humans rebel and try to take back the love they feel they have lost in the form of rape or child molestation. But this doesn't satisfy them, as they cannot feel the love in acts forced upon others. Others shut down their love completely, never allowing themselves to love themselves or another, and become grumpy old men and women at the end of their lives. Then there are those who do the best they can with the contradiction and live a lie between their feelings and behaviour. Some remain completely confused for all of their lives and never fully recover.

As you can see, it is not surprising that humans have difficulties with sex and other forms of physical love. We are here to offer help.

The first step *is to understand that you are not alone. There* *is not one person on the planet who is not confused about sex and physical love.*

The second step *is to learn to love yourself. We are not just talking here about masturbation, although that is one form of self-love, generally. Here we talk about emotional love for self.*

When you have grown up feeling guilty for sexual feelings that are frowned upon by society, you end up with little emotional self-love. Even those who have learned to love themselves physically, often have not learned to love themselves emotionally because of the guilt that they carry.

It is possible to change your society one step at a time, but for now, you all have to live in the society into which you were born, and to a certain extent, abide by its rules.

But you can start by speaking out about the problems which your society's stance on sex and physical love has caused. You can also begin to learn to love yourself, both emotionally and physically.

Once you have learned to love yourself, you can take the love you experience, and share it with another. As you learned before, even a hug allows you to honour your feelings.

Often humans find it easier to hug their pets than they do their immediate family. This is all due to the confusion that people feel about sharing their love with others and they know their pets won't complain.

One reason that humans don't share their love in physical ways such as a hug, is that they fear that the other person may not want a hug. In the society you have created, a hug can make someone feel uncomfortable due to your society's programming, not from their natural instincts. It also is dependent on the reason the hug is offered.

As humans are empathic, they can feel if a hug is given unwillingly or as an extension of the person's love. It is always important to follow your feelings, and only give a hug when it is an extension of your love. You will have more success when you have learned to love yourself emotionally and physically.

We can help you with this.

In the meantime, as you learn to love yourself and extend your love to others, it may be beneficial to always ask the other person if they would like a hug (or whatever form of physical love you would like to extend) to be sure not to offend.

But if you follow your feelings, you will know if the other person is open to an extension of your love by the way you feel. This does take some practice, so in the beginning, it would be safest to always ask. Also, it would be beneficial to talk of love and sex often, to allow your society to be more open about the subject. Don't worry about being embarrassed; you are no more embarrassed than anyone else and the more you talk about it, the more you can talk about it.

Life was meant to be enjoyed. Your bodies were meant to be enjoyed. If you can learn to love yourself first, and extend your love out to others, you have a much better chance of enjoying your life and your body.

Changes on the Planet

We wanted to tell you about life on Earth. We wanted to talk to you about the progress of life on your planet.

It's so exciting that everything is happening just as it was planned. All is well. You have no need to fear any changes that are happening on your planet. All is happening for the good of the All.

We are excited to share with you that critical mass is not very far away. All of the remaining dark features of your planet will begin to crumble as the light pierces through the darkness.

Don't worry if things seem to be in a state of upheaval. This was to be expected. All is well, and everyone on this side is super excited.

We will have further instructions for you, to help you navigate the changes that are coming. Don't worry. Keep focused on love, and all will be well.

Helping Bring about the New Age

Lorelle, we talked about love, about life after death, and life on Earth. We haven't talked to you about life in the New Spirituality, the New Age that is coming to your planet.

You know that this age is getting closer every day. You know that all of you light workers are working hard to bring this age into being. So are we angels. We are all one, with a common goal. Our goal is to recreate the Earth as a world filled with love.

Originally, it was created that way, but humans decided they wanted to understand the difference between good and evil, so you were allowed to create evil on this planet so that you would better understand what is good. You were able to experience fear, so that you could better understand love.

Now we are drawing close to the time when fear will be replaced by love, and evil will be replaced by good. You will have no more need to experience evil and fear, because you now understand the difference.

We are coming up to an exciting time when everyone will awaken to the fact that there is no separation between yourselves and God, between each other as well. It is so exciting to know that soon you will look at your neighbour and see yourself, and you will look at someone whom you previously thought of as evil, and understand that, just like you, they have the same capacity to be good.

Lorelle, we are celebrating now with our music and joyful sounds, as we all move closer to the day when love will rule your planet, when we angels and you humans will be in constant open contact with each other. Love will be felt all over the planet, and shared amongst all humans, and between the realms openly and freely. Love will become the dominant force in every human's life.

You can all help to bring this New Age closer more quickly, by communicating with your angels regularly, by meditating often, by thinking love as much as possible, by living in the moment, and by sharing your love with all you meet, and out into the world.

What a glorious day it will be when love rules the world, and angels and humans work together to make love the dominant force on your planet. You are love. We are love. Let's share our love with each other and with all the world.

❋❋❋

Shining Light on Your Shadows

Lorelle, we wanted to talk to you today to tell you the future of your planet.

Everyone has been talking about ascension and ascension symptoms, and this is what is happening on your planet at this time, but there is more going on than is spoken about. We are all working to bring about the future that you have been praying for—the Earth where love rules, peace reigns, and everyone is treated with respect.

There is a lot happening on your side, and on ours. All of the light workers, as you call them, are working hard to bring light and love to the physical side, and to wake people up to the light that dwells within each person.

On our side, we are providing what help we are allowed to your efforts, but we are also helping by changing the structure of the way light and dark interact on your planet.

Now that you all understand the meaning of dark and light, and the difference between the two, there is no reason to keep all of the darkness on your planet. Many of those who were considered to be shrouded in darkness are beginning to see the light in others, and to awaken to the light within themselves. There is now no need for darkness to remain on your planet in such large quantities. It is time to let go of the darkness within yourselves, so that the light can overwhelm it.

You are right in what you were thinking: you can embrace your shadow side, because, once you first acknowledge your shadows, it is then like you have shone your light on your shadows, and they, too, become light. You can use all of your resources to help bring more light to the planet.

Whilst you still have shadows that you hide within you, the light cannot overcome it.

How can we find our shadows within?

First, you have to acknowledge that you have them.

I am guessing that if we didn't have shadows, we wouldn't be on this Earth.

That is not always true, Lorelle. Some people are pure light, embodied in order to help bring more light to your planet, but chances are that most people reading this will have shadows that they need to acknowledge and release. In order to find your shadows, there are a number of ways.

The first is to ask and you shall receive. If you ask for us to show your shadows to you, you will become aware of them. It is best to do this during meditation, and to tackle one shadow at a time.

You are right that Debbie Ford's online course[8] is still one of the best resources for tackling your shadows.

Once you reveal the darkness that dwells within yourself, you start to shed light on it. Light will always overcome the darkness. Sometimes the darkness will return, however, if the original source of that darkness is not examined. This is why the course you did was so beneficial, as it allowed you to follow your shadow where it led you—to the source, and to then shed light all along the way.

Once your light has overcome your shadows, you have more resources to help bring peace, love, and light to your planet. Don't worry about how to do this at the moment. Your angels and guides are helping to show you your shadows and to overcome them, particularly if you ask for this specific help.

As you have discovered, sometimes there are different layers of darkness. You might get rid of the really dark layer, and think that you have completely exposed that shadow, only to find that there are less dark, slightly more subtle shadows underneath.

Remember that you are peace and love. To bring peace and love to your planet, you just have to remove those things that are blocking your true self from sharing its light with the world.

Once the majority of people have begun to peel away the layers of darkness, more and more light will shine into the world. More peace will be experienced. More love will be experienced.

❋❋❋

Consider the Consequences to All That Is

Lorelle, you know that we have talked about many things and many of them have been related to love. Even those you thought were not about love, like war, were related to love, and you know that the reason is because all of God's creation is love.

But today we wanted to talk to you about something entirely different. We wanted to talk to you about life on your planet.

You know that life on your planet is threatened by the effects that humans are having on the environment. You have also learned that Mother Earth is a powerful being who would not allow life on her, or her life, to cease, so she gives you all sorts of pointers as to how you can change your ways. And as you learned from the fairies, the best thing you can do for all on your planet is to consider the consequences of all of your actions and thoughts.

But remember that you have much help in all this. If you ask for help to find a way to honour your planet and all who live on her, and help to consider the consequences of all you think, say and do, we will assist you.

As you were just thinking, some of you do remember to consider the consequences of what you do, even if it is in hindsight. But sometimes you cannot think of a way to do things where the consequences are positive instead of negative. We can help with that as well. We can help you come up with ideas of ways to improve the conditions for all the beings on the planet, including yourselves. But first you need to ask for help.

You all have free will, and we honour the free will of every being on the planet. God has put in place a system in this universe to allow every being's desires to come to them, even though your desires may be mutually exclusive. It can take a little longer when your desires are diametrically opposed, but everyone's free will is respected.

The task ahead is to get more people to a) believe that the Earth is in danger, and b) do something about it.

The first answer is pray. You can pray for help with all these things, and help is at hand. You can pray for help with convincing people, with fixing the problems. Help with everything is at hand, once you ask for it.

Faith that all will be well is also a key ingredient. Have faith that God has allowed you free will and that God has allowed you the ability to achieve all of your desires. The more people who desire a world where all of life is respected, the more quickly it will come about. Have faith and all will be well.

Don't worry if things look a little dark at present, and if the people in power don't seem to be listening. God created you in his spiritual image, and as such, you are powerful beings. Have faith in yourselves as powerful beings as well. You can be, do, and have whatever you desire. If you all, or the majority of you, desire a world where all life is respected, where Mother Earth is respected, you must achieve that. It is the law.

What about when others desire that we don't achieve our desires, because they don't want to lose the power they have?

They think they have the power, but you are all powerful, regardless of who controls the army, the banks, the money markets, or the lawmakers. You have the power to achieve your aims. Believe and it is so. Ask and you shall receive.

❊❊❊

Time to Shine Your Light

Lorelle, thank you for being a voice for the angels, and for the animals and others for whom you speak out, including Mother Earth. We are here now to tell you how you can help Mother Earth and all the animals on the planet.

You are love, as are all of the humans on the planet, but

many humans don't know what they are, and haven't learned to act that way. You have learned what you are and have been endeavouring to be the love that you are. It takes practice, and you know that sometimes you need examples of other people who have gone before you, who have shown you how to be the love that you are. There are many examples, and you have thought of a few: Jesus, Gandhi, Martin Luther King, and these are all wonderful examples of people living as love in difficult circumstances.

Lorelle, you find yourself in challenging circumstances now, as the world is now changing rapidly. It is time to be the example of the love that you are. Not just you personally, but all of you humans who have learned that you are love.

How can you be that example?

You are doing it now to a limited extent, by sharing information on Facebook, and by sharing your loving card readings. But each one of you now has to stand up for love in the world.

You know that in the past, when people say that you have to stand up for something or someone, it has meant that you need to confront something opposed to that for which you stand. And although that is not really the case here, there will be those who oppose you and your action as a voice for love, because not all humans have embraced their love and the love of others.

Although all humans are searching for love to a certain extent, not all humans understand that they don't need to search for it, because they are love, as is all other parts of God's creation.

As you learned, what you give, you receive. To experience the love that you are, it is better to give love and you can then experience not only the love you give, but also the love you receive in return.

Each of you has been given unique divine gifts designed for your unique divine mission to bring more love into the world. We are here to help all of you with the courage and the skills required to carry out your roles.

We are all working together this end to help you bring about the world of your dreams, and this is one reason we didn't want to tell you the names of the angels you are talking to. It is time for all humanity also to work together with our help to achieve the desires of all.

Messages from God

Step out of Your Comfort Zone

Your angels told you that you will need to emerge from your comfort zone and be more instrumental as an example of love. You wonder how you will go about that, but you don't need to worry about that at the moment.

We, your angels and I, know that each of you is facing new situations that you have never faced before. You are receiving a lot of help from your spiritual helpers, but it is still challenging for each of you, as you are feeling like you are walking out into the darkness without a light to see where you are going. But your light is within, and the light from your spiritual helpers is helping to light your path for you.

You each have a unique path to walk, and you each have help on the path and to light the way for you, but each of you can only walk your path alone. All of humanity is finding their way at the moment, not quite knowing where you are heading, and that can be a scary experience for you all. But many like you have faith that all will be well, and your faith will see you through. Your love will see you through.

Don't worry about how to find your way when you don't know where you are heading. You are all used to travelling with a map in hand. This form of travel is from the known to the unknown. The unknown can be scary even if you know that all will be well in the end.

Don't worry. Hold onto your joy even as you feel your way through the unknown and unseen parts of your journey.

With faith and love, you will come through ok. We will help you follow the paths you chose before you incarnated. Yes, some of you have reassessed your paths in recent times, but your higher selves, angels, and spirit guides are all aware of where you need to be at this time and are helping you to find your path and remain on the right path.

Love will see you through, but don't worry if you fail to be as loving as you would desire to be all the time. It can be stressful to be in such challenging circumstances with changes happening all around you. This is one reason why it is important to have regular meditation sessions to release the stress you have built up. If others are not as loving as you would hope at this time, please make allowances for the stress that everyone is facing. Send them love to help them to remember the love that they are, and they may be able to release the stress they carry.

I am with you always, as are Jesus and other Ascended Masters. Everyone on this side is doing their best to help you to be the love that you are, in order for you to bring about the world that you desire.

Don't worry about the fear that some are feeling. That is just fear of the unknown, but there is also fear of losing your freedom as some of you have experienced during the COVID pandemic. Know that as children of God, you are love; you are joy; you are peace, and you are freedom. There is no way for anyone to take away your freedom, unless you allow them to.

You may lose some physical freedom, but you are still free to be the love that you are, and you are still free to be peace and joy.

Can you now step into the roles that your souls have assigned for you? Your angels and guides will help you to find and carry out those roles, but don't forget to ask for help. You each chose your assigned role, and each desired to achieve that role on your own, but you have much help. Your guides and angels can let you know what they can help you with and what you have chosen to achieve on your own.

Meditating regularly will help you keep in touch with your higher self, who will let you know the next step you need to take, and your spiritual helpers will be there to assist you.

You are becoming the humans that you desire to be. You are becoming those beings who desire to experience being the love that they are and to experience the knowledge that all of my creation is made of love.

We are one. You and all of humanity are one with me, one with the angels, one with your guides, with the Ascended Masters, with the rest of humanity, with the animals, the plants, the trees, the Earth.

All of the beings on your planet and all of the beings on the spiritual planes will rejoice as you step forward into your roles of being the love that you are. There will be much rejoicing on this side and on the physical side as life takes a giant leap towards the world of your dreams, where peace reigns, love rules, and everyone is treated with respect.

Be prepared for major changes to come rapidly now. Be

prepared for some people to be very afraid of those rapid changes. Show compassion to those who struggle to adapt to the changes. Remember that everyone is doing the best they can.

Love yourself during this process and you will find it easier to love others. For as you learned, without loving yourself first, you can't experience the love you wish to share. Be the best that you can be, and you will be that example of love that the angels spoke to you about.

Don't worry about how this will all play out. There is a grand plan, and you would be absolutely amazed if you knew it all. There is not one person on the planet who has been given the entire picture of what is now unfolding for your planet, so you don't need to feel as though you have been left out. Some have a little more information to help them step into their roles, but no one there knows it all. There is a reason for this.

As circumstances change so rapidly, the desires of each human has an effect on how changes play out. This is one very good reason to maintain a positive outlook, and to avoid too much negativity at this time. Devote your efforts to your assigned roles without wasting your efforts on trying to understand all that is happening. The world is changing so rapidly that your understanding cannot keep up.

Focus on the roles your souls have chosen for you. Keep love in your hearts and on your minds, and envisage the world of your dreams. Be love, think love, and act with love and all will be well.

Love is the answer to all questions. Ask and you shall receive. If you need more love, think love. If you need even more love, just ask.

You know love will prevail and there is nothing to fear in this world or the next. Some people may leave this world, this plane, but you know that that is just a transition to another world where love rules and peace reigns. There is nothing to fear.

Be at peace.

Can you be at peace, when all around chaos ensues? Yes, you can. You are peace. Go within to find the peace that you are. All around you is peace as well. You can find peace in nature, but remember that peace comes from within; the peace in nature merely reminds you of the peace within you. If you can't find your peace, ask for help and it will be given.

Go now and be the peace that you are, the love that you are, the joy that you are, and the freedom that you are. We are here to help you be that, but know that you are a child of God, come to Earth with all those attributes in order to experience yourself as that. You cannot fail.

Don't hide your light but allow it to shine for all to see. Allow your light to shine on your path to God. Others will see your light and know that they too have a light to shine on their own unique path to God. God rests within each of you.

Don't be afraid of the dark. You have sufficient light within you to drive out the darkness from the entire planet. With each of you shining your light in the darkness, no more darkness will be experienced. There may be still a few shadows remaining, but with all the light that you all are producing, those shadows will soon be exposed and become light as well.

I am with you always, always available to talk to, to help you, to share your worries and joys, your failures and triumphs. Call on me at any time for help. Call on your angels, your guides, and your other spiritual helpers. We are all here to ensure that your transition to the new world happens as seamlessly as possible.

I will be with you through all eternity. For you are all eternal beings, and there is no hurry for you to achieve your aims. You can take many lifetimes if you wish. But if it is your desire to create the world of your dreams in the shortest time possible, then each of you will have to step up now, to step into your roles as quickly as possible.

Let us know what you desire, and we can help you achieve your desires, but you are magical creative beings who can create miracles, just as Jesus did. Have faith in yourself as children of God. Have faith in God and all of your helpers. Have faith, too, in your fellow humans. While each one of you has unique abilities, each of you also has the same creative abilities to help create the world of your dreams.

Don't forget to ask for help.

Now you have no need to worry about your future. Your future is assured as eternal beings. Rest easily in the present moment, where your love, peace, joy, and freedom are more easily experienced.

Just as love is all there is, the present moment is all there is, and this is why you find your love in the present moment. Embrace your love and embrace the present moment, and you have nothing to fear.

I love you and want only the best for you. You have desired a world filled with love, but it will take a lot of you to bring about that world—a lot of you being that example of love to others.

Now is the time for all humans to be the change they wish to see. If you desire a more peaceful world, be peace—focus on the peace that dwells within you and share it with the world. If you desire a world with more love, be the love that you are—focus on the love that dwells within you and share it with all you meet, send it out into the world, not only to the humans, but to all of the creatures and Mother Earth herself.

Now that you are all endeavouring to be the love that you are, the world of your dreams will become a reality in no time.

To create the world of your dreams, you may also need to take action. To be the change you want to see, you can't just walk past the litter on the ground and expect someone else to pick it up. You can't just walk past the injustice in the world and expect someone else to bring justice to that situation.

I know that some of you feel like you don't have any power, but you are powerful beings created in the spiritual likeness of God. God doesn't have a physical likeness, except as my creation, but I am a powerful creator, and I have created all of you as powerful creative beings also.

Ask and you shall receive. But if you wish to receive the world of your dreams as quickly as possible, the more action steps you can take towards that world, the quicker it will come to you. You can all work together to bring about this amazing, wonderful, loving, peaceful world you desire. The first step is to recognise your power, and that power comes from your love. Your love comes from my love. We are one.

Now that you know you are powerful, you may be tempted to wield that power against others, but the power of love is not power over, but power with. This power works best when it is used in conjunction with the love of all those you aim to influence.

You can move forward now into your roles that the angels spoke of, knowing you can have the confidence of a creative, powerful child of God. You are a spiritual being having a physical experience, and your spiritual being is made in the likeness of God, your creator. You are my child, one with God, one with all of my creation. I can help you to experience that oneness if you ask me. Once you are aware of your oneness and have experienced it, you will never look at the rest of my creation as anything other than one with you, and one with God.

Now that you have learned of your oneness with All That Is, it will be so much easier to make allowances for those who are still sleeping. Those of you who are awake can work together to bring more light into the world, and that light might remind the sleeping ones of the light and love within themselves.

Now that you are aware of all the help you have, there is no reason for you not to take that first brave step out of your comfort zone. That first step may seem hard at first, but you will look back and realise that you were born for this and it wasn't so hard after all. Then you will be ready for the next brave step. Take one small brave step at a time, and you will reach your goals in no time.

Love goes with you wherever you go. Rely on that love. Rest in that love and you will know there is nothing to fear in this world or the next.

Now, my beloveds, you are ready. You are ready to be a beacon of the love and light which dwells within each one of you. You are ready to shine your light out into the world. You are ready to be the love that you are in all that you think, say, and do.

I am proud of each one of you, and you can be proud of yourself as you take those small brave steps towards the world of your dreams.

Go now and be my beacon of light and love to all the world

❈❈❈

Moving Forward to a New Earth

Now that we have talked about all the things that people are and what they need to do to bring about the New Earth, everyone will have the confidence to become the people they are destined to be. There may be some preparatory steps before people embark upon a new life in their new role.

Some people are already well on the way towards their roles, whereas others are just beginning. For each one though, there is still a comfort zone you need to step out of. You take one step forward, become comfortable, and then take another step forward, or a leap of faith for some. While you are all ready for your next steps towards your roles, some have more steps to take before they can fully embrace them.

Those steps may be difficult for some. It may involve looking back to where you have been, seeing which of those steps led you in the right direction and which led you away from your goals. It may involve looking back to your childhood and noticing the events which shaped your behaviours and your beliefs. You may need to forgive some people who have hurt you, but when you look at the situation from their perspective, you will come to understand why they did what they did. With understanding, forgiveness may not seem necessary, but forgiveness allows you release those past hurts which may be holding you back from your leap of faith.

Some people may need professional help to come to terms with past hurts and to move forward. These actions are liberating, because they allow you to let go of the past and focus on the present, where your peace, love, joy and freedom reside.

Have faith in yourself and your ability to move past any old hurts. If you ask for help, your spiritual helpers can help you find the perfect help to allow you to let go of the past and move forward.

Life is richer for those who can let go of the anger, bitterness and pain dragging them backwards. These deep-seated emotions are like being chained to heavy weights. Any movement forward is limited by those weights. Once you can release past hurts, these heavy weights and the chains are released. You are free to fly and move forward with ease.

Freedom may take some getting used to. You are accustomed to carrying those weights and may have to make adjustments, so you don't become disoriented as you move forward with ease.

Life in the New Earth

Now let us talk about what it will be like when the New Earth comes into being. We spoke about that and the future of religions on this planet in your previous book, WE ARE ONE. As the New Earth comes into being in the near future, the timing of the changes is largely dependent on each one of you, and how easily and quickly you can work together to help bring about the New Earth.

Your experience of the New Earth will be love-ly; the Earth and everyone on the planet will be filled with love. As you know, all of my creation is love already, but when the New Earth comes into being, everyone will know they are love. When humans know they are love and continue to act that way, they will allow all of my creation to be the love they are as well.

As you were just thinking, Lorelle, this is just your planet we are referring to here. Other planets are already acting as love, and some are a long way off that. But the Earth will become a place where love rules and peace reigns and everyone is treated with respect.

"What will this look like?" you may be wondering.

It will look like whatever you imagine it to look like. You are created as creative children of God. I have given each of you the ability to create the world that you desire, given enough faith and love.

So how do you imagine a world that is filled with love to be? I can give you some ideas.

Perhaps you would like a world where no one is allowed to starve to death. You know that each person incarnates into the circumstances they have planned prior to birth, and you may wonder if you would be denying those people their destined life of poverty and starvation if you helped them. But what if the only reason they have come to Earth in such a situation is so that they can give you the opportunity to help them?

So the answer to what the world would be like may not be so easy to imagine. The only thing that you can do is to follow your feelings: the voice of your soul.

Your soul knows what it and any souls it encounters have

come here to experience. Follow your feelings and you will know whether it is right to help someone or not. It may sound harsh not to help someone who you think is in need of help, but what if they came into that situation with the aim of learning to help themselves? I am not just talking about that person who is starving, but any situation you encounter.

It is not your role to judge others or the life they have been born into. It is your role to follow your feelings and to be the best person you can be. The best person you can be is the person who allows others to follow their feelings also, and to make their own choices.

You know that to be the best person you can be, you need to think love, be love and act with love in all that you do. You can ask: "What would love do now?" if you are unsure.

Love may not always act to change another's lifestyle, because that lifestyle may be what they have chosen for their life. As you were just thinking, Lorelle, some people in the past have made that mistake when they encountered Indigenous people, who they thought were living inferior lives as savages. Colonisers tore families apart and enforced civilisation upon them and caused great harm in the process. Even though they were acting with love, their actions were not, in fact, loving actions, because they failed to consider the others' point of view.

So, when you consider the future that you would like to create on this New Earth which is coming to your planet, remember that you need to follow your feelings here too. When you imagine a New Earth, imagine a world that makes you feel joyful. Your joy is a sign that your soul is pleased by your imaginings. We can help you here too.

If you are uncertain of the world you desire, just ask to create a world that is in the best interests of All That Is, and ask for all of your imaginings and all of your actions to help create that world.

Love is the answer to all questions and love will help you create the world of your dreams, but don't forget that you can ask for help.

❈❈❈

Messages from the Angels

Influencing Others

As God told you, there are a lot of changes happening now. No one on the planet understands all that is happening. Even we angels concern ourselves with our own area of interest only and allow others to see to theirs. We are asking you all to work together to bring about the world that you desire, but you know that each one of you has unique gifts which allow you to fulfil your role. You don't need to know what another person's role is, or what their special gifts are. You only need to focus on your own area of expertise and those who fall within your concern.

You sometimes worry that others are not doing their part or are not be as committed to the changes as you are. This may be true, but as you learned, Lorelle, you cannot change what other people do or think by pushing against it. You can influence only with love, and by example.

Don't allow your worry about others to deflect you from your path, from your role.

Now that each of you is focused on your unique role in the world, the changes will begin to happen more rapidly. I know some of you still feel like you don't know what your role is as you move towards the New Earth, but you can receive all the information you require from your higher self and your spiritual helpers during meditation. You will be shown one step at a time so as not to overwhelm you.

I know you like to plan for the future, and where future planning is required, sufficient information will be given to you. However, there is no point in attempting to learn all about every aspect of your future, because, as God informed you, not every aspect has been agreed upon yet.

As you were told, asking for all of your thoughts, words and deeds to be based on love, and to be for the greater good of All That Is, ensures that your influence is heading the world in the direction you desire.

If you desire others to use their influence to also head the world in that direction, the only way is by sending them love, and by becoming a shining light for all to see, as you lead the way towards that New Earth. But don't expect others to follow your path exactly, as every path is different. You are all children of God, all with a shining light within, ready to help bring about the New Earth in your own unique way.

However, if you wish to allow others to see the light within you, in order to bring more light into the world so that they will see their light within and bring more light into the world, you may need to take down some barriers to that light.

Removing Shadows

As you were told previously, it is necessary not to hide your light under a bushel basket, which means not to knowingly block the light that you are emitting into the world. But you may also be blocking the light unknowingly.

You can block your light by allowing your ego to take control of your life. Your ego thinks there is danger everywhere and likes to hide from that danger. In order to hide from danger, your ego may be getting you to block your light.

Your shadows can also block your light. They were accumulated during your life, mostly during your childhood, and have become habits which stop you from experiencing and expressing your love. When you stop expressing love, you are focused elsewhere—on your shadow or on another's. Once you look at your shadow with love, it disappears. But you need to focus on love first.

As you learned, Lorelle, there are programs available online to allow you to identify and eliminate your shadows. But everyone is different, and everyone may need to tackle those shadows in different ways. Staying in touch with your higher self and spiritual helpers will allow you to know the best course of action for each of you.

God has given each of you many gifts, and some of those gifts are your emotions, which are energy in motion. Those emotions lead you to feelings in your body and those feelings lead you to act in a certain way.

It is necessary to uncover your emotions, to allow your feelings to be felt in their fullness, in order to use those emotions and feelings in accordance with your unique gifts.

Whilst your ego is ruling your life, those emotions and feelings are rarely understood, and rarely result in the outcome for which they were gifted to you. Learning to understand your shadows, your emotions, and your feelings is essential if you are to carry out your role at this time. Your spiritual helpers can help you with all of these things if you ask them.

Now that you have uncovered your shadows and released your emotions, you may become temporarily overwhelmed. It is likely that you have suppressed your emotions for such a long time that, once they are released, they may explode out of you. Be kind to yourself at this time, but also be kind to others. If possible, warn your immediate family that you are working on some personal issues at the moment, and if you are seen to be angry or crying, do not fret, because this is just part of the process, and once released, these emotions will be better understood and better controlled.

The other thing to remember is that shadows often come in layers. You may release one shadow and think you are free of all shadows, only to find that there are others lurking under that layer. Further work may be required at a later time, but if you stay in touch with your higher self and spiritual helpers, we will keep you on the right track.

Others' Reaction to Your Light

Now that your shadows are diminished, your light may become more noticeable to others. Others who are still living in the dark may respond in different ways to your bright light.

Your light may be so bright that it overwhelms others. They may think you have changed and that you are trying to change them. For those hiding in the darkness, change can feel like a threat. Be kind to everyone and allow them to react to your light in their own ways without being insistent that they also shine their light. Also, avoid the temptation to cover your light to make it easier for others to accept you. Your light is what will allow you to fulfil your role. Covering it will impede your progress.

Another reaction that others may have to your strong light is mistrust. How can others trust you when you are so different from them, and perhaps so different to the person you used to be when you were hiding in the dark? You can assure others of your integrity, but you cannot convince anyone who doesn't want to be convinced. By your fruits will they know you. Ensure that your fruits are always good and lead by example.

Some will react to your light by being intrigued, by wanting to find out more about you and where your light is coming from. Please instruct them that you are not unique in that sense. Yes, each person has unique gifts, but everyone has an equal measure of light within, which you can all shine as brightly if you wish.

There will be some who think that your bright light means that you are the chosen one. You need to assure them that they, too, are special. That they, too, have the same light within them and just need to allow it to shine forth. Yes, they may need a few preparatory steps, but they, too, can shine as brightly.

Be sure to keep your feet firmly on the ground. Don't allow others to build you up to be greater than they are. Everyone has a unique role, but none of you is greater or lesser than any other. If you begin to believe you are greater or better, your spiritual helpers will find a way to bring you back down to Earth, so to speak, and that may not be pleasant for you. Even though you may be shining more brightly at the moment, everyone is equal, and everyone has an equal capacity to be brilliant.

Now that you understand your roles and you have taken steps to remove your shadows and move forward, some of you will become leaders. Whilst their spiritual helpers will endeavour to keep them seeing themselves as equals, you may need to help with that, if it becomes necessary. A gentle reminder should be all that is required.

Now go and shine your light out into the world, and help bring about the changes you desire.

❄❄❄

Messages from God

Different Perspectives on Truth

God, my communication with you led me to believe that those parts of the Bible which talk about necromancy and other spiritual gifts being sinful were added by the church, and were not the word of God. A spiritual teacher, who has a strong connection with you as far as appearances go, says she believes that it is the word of God now, that it is a sin to do those things.

I know, Lorelle. You know that the only true reality is love, and you know that both she and you speak with love in relation to these things. You therefore believe that you should believe the same thing. But what if I told you that God's plan for each of you is different, even though God loves each of you equally.

Most people believe that the truth is the truth, regardless of whose it is.

I know. As you know, God's perspective is different through every physical being, even though God's perspective through Ultimate Reality is the same for everyone and everything—

absolute love. I see the world differently through your eyes than through the other person's, because you both have different reasons for being, even though both of these reasons are to be love, think love, and act with love in all that you do.

When she thinks love, she thinks the Bible is the ultimate truth. When you think love, you think that your ultimate truth comes from God within. As in many questions, these are not either/or answers, but both/and.

At the time of the Bible being changed to reflect the fact that certain attributes were a sin, it was a necessary step for the evolution of man. Now it is a necessary step for the evolution of man to understand that, regardless of anyone's beliefs, you can still love each other. You can respect each other's beliefs as being the truth for them, and unable to affect you in any way.

What about those followers of Islam who believe that only their way is right, and everyone else needs to be eradicated?

Lorelle, your book, WE ARE ONE, *allowed followers of Islam to see that there can be other perspectives of Islam than those proposed centuries ago, and the new perspectives are no more wrong than the old ones.*

Most people need to believe that there is only one absolute truth.

Yes, Lorelle. There is—love. And when you allow love to rule your life, rather than the words of another being, whether they be a well-respected author, a prophet, or the so-called written word of God, you are always acting from the source of absolute truth.

As you learned before, love is the answer to all questions. Love will conquer the world. Love will understand that conquering doesn't mean eradicating or controlling. Love means allowing, accepting, forgiving, and understanding. Love means freedom, peace, and joy, and denying anyone their right to freedom, peace, and joy is not love.

❄❄❄

Does Evil Exist?

We had a conversation at our New Spirituality Study Group meeting the other day about good and evil. Is there evil in the world?

There is a perception of evil in the world, Lorelle. Remember that nothing is either good or bad lest thinking makes it so.

And is there a devil?

Not in the sense that people believe. There are entities who have less than honourable intentions, but like the evil in this world, it is a matter of perception.

First of all, there is no perception in the spirit world, is there? I thought that was only on the Earth, where there is up and down, etc.—duality.

No, Lorelle. There is perception on all planes. Some people perceive themselves to be still in a physical body, even when they are in spirit. Some people, who are in spirit and have less than honourable intentions, could be perceived as devils or demons.

Is there a fallen angel in charge of all dark forces?

No, Lorelle. Lorelle it is not in your best interests to know everything that goes on in spirit but suffice to say: I am in charge of everything, even those things perceived to be evil. But that is not to say that I condone what you perceive to be evil; only that I allow everyone to have free will.

If we send all of these entities love, will love conquer evil? Can the dark forces become light in this way?

If we are to know what is good, we first have to know what is bad. In other words, we can't get rid of all the duality in all parts of time and space, because then there would be no knowledge of good and evil.

Would we not be back to the Garden of Eden then?

No, Lorelle. There is no going back; only forward to a new Earth, a new age of peace and love.

I am a bit confused.

I know. This is why it is not in your best interests to know more about this. You cannot understand all of it from your limited perception there on Earth.

God is in charge of it all. God cares for all of creation but allows every being to have free will—the will to choose between good and evil or anywhere in between.

I feel like there is more information that I need before I can put this to rest.

I know, Lorelle, and you shall have that information at another time.

The Son of God

God, you know I have finished reading that spiritual teacher's book[9] about her transformation from an angel lady to a strict follower of Jesus. You know I felt confused, as it led me on a rollercoaster of emotions—anger, sadness, love, and a bit of fear.

I don't know quite what to make of it. Can you help me?

Not really, Lorelle. You have made a connection with God, without going through Jesus, even though you love and respect Jesus. The author you speak of only found her connection with God after finding Jesus, so she really does think of Jesus as her saviour, which he is in that sense.

But I really don't understand, and never have been able to, how Jesus can have died for our sins.

I know, Lorelle.

Is that something that you can help me with?

No, Lorelle. Jesus didn't die. Just like all of you, he had eternal life. Your eternal life didn't start with the death of Jesus, but perhaps your awareness of it did. You can understand the concept of eternal life more easily, following Jesus' example of life after death.

I have asked before, I think, about Jesus' sonship. Is Jesus the only Son of God, as part of the trinity?

No, Lorelle. You are all part of the Sonship. Jesus is the figurehead of the Sonship, but you are all Jesus' brothers and sisters, all children of God.

Fallen Angels

God, was Jesus with you in the beginning?

Not Jesus per se, Lorelle, but the Word from which Jesus sprang, from which you all sprang. It is not Jesus, but all humans who I gave dominion over the angels. As your myth tells you, the angels were asked to be subject to humankind, and the fallen angels refused to submit. There are elements of truth to this myth, but it is not true in the way it has been understood.

The story is told that God is on one side, and Satan is on the other, and humans in between, deciding who to be loyal to. This tale is not true.

As I said, it is not in your best interests to know everything, but suffice to say that I allowed some angels to become equal with humans. In doing so, I allowed them to understand the trials and tribulations humans endure, and some of them thought they could find better ways for humans to overcome these trials, other than turning to God.

However, the main battle in this world is not between the forces of good and evil, but between the ego mind and the God mind in humans. The ego does listen to the ways of those offering alternative means to achieve happiness, but the ego is a gift from God. Even the fallen angels, as they are called, are a gift from God.

Just as in the story of the Friendly Soul, the fallen angels are there to offer you choices, to offer you a way other than God's way. Although God only leads you to love, God does allow you to know something less than love, so that you can recognise love when you feel it. God also offers you a way to feel only love, if that is your desire.

The Bible

From what I read in that book, it doesn't sound like the Bible is a way to find only love.

No, Lorelle. The Bible offers you a choice of perspectives. Just as you refused to be influenced by the God of Wrath of the Old

Testament, and only follow Jesus' teachings of love, others have taken other parts of the Bible to find their paths to follow.

According to this author, we should follow all of the teachings of the Bible.

If you did that, Lorelle, you would be continually changing, because the messages of The Bible are many and varied.

So, God, what about Jesus suffering for our sins, even if he didn't die?

Yes, Lorelle, Jesus did suffer, but it was his choice, always. Free will is paramount. But just as you have at times submitted to my will, Jesus did at the time of his suffering, allowing himself to be an example to all humans. He intended for everyone to understand that it matters not what others do or say; you can overcome any difficulties with God's help, and no matter what, your life is eternal. The message has been somewhat skewed, though.

Our Sins

But how do our sins come into it?

They don't, Lorelle. In the eyes of God, everyone is sinless. Sin is a choice offered by the fallen angels. There is no such thing as sin in God's world, where love rules.

So Jesus' suffering on the cross doesn't change the way we are viewed by God, or the way that our transgressions are viewed?

No, Lorelle. God sees only love.

What about when we act in unloving ways?

You know, Lorelle, we discussed that when you act in unloving ways to one part of God's creation, you are generally acting in loving ways towards another, or at least believing that you are.

The Grand Plan

So, is there a grand plan, firstly with that book?

Not in the way that you think, Lorelle.

With the author's conversion?

Everything happens in divine order, but God doesn't dictate all activities, as all beings have free will. I just order the pieces. However, if you think love, be love, and act with love in all that you do, you are acting according to my divine plan, because this is my will—to be love, think love, and act with love.

But everyone's perspective of love is different, isn't it?

The closer you come to Ultimate Reality of love, unconditional love, the closer your perspective is to others who are also close to unconditional love.

Is there a grand plan in the world?

Yes, Lorelle, and you are helping plan it. You are my child, and you help to create the world around you, but I keep order so that when your aim is love, love is your outcome.

God, that book and now our conversation has left me troubled, even though I have felt joy in the communication.

I know, Lorelle. You are troubled because you had a joyful, childlike view of the world, and you allowed the author of that book and I to come and tell you that Santa doesn't exist. There's no going back from that; only forward.
You don't need Santa to be happy, Lorelle. You don't need a world where there is no such thing as evil.
I know you hoped that the world would become one where peace would reign, and love would rule, and that is still possible. Even though there is still evil in the world, if you and enough of your fellow-humans can be love, think love, and act with love in all that you do, and you all focus on the loving world you wish to create, you are sure to achieve that, because it is God's will.

God, Thy will be done.

And yours, Lorelle.

(I was troubled after reading the book[10] by the once well-respected teacher and author of classes and books about angel card reading and interacting with spiritual beings, as she had suddenly denounced all of her previous beliefs and teachings. The troubled feeling left me when I picked up my ebook to read, and was surprised to find *A Course In Miracles*[11] open there, considering I hadn't looked at that book for years. Thank you God and Jesus for making me understand that you are always there for me and that miracles happen every day.)

❆❆❆

Animal Welfare

Lorelle, what would you like to talk about?

Well, God, the only thing on my mind is Tiki (our 12 week old Doberman puppy).

I know, Lorelle. She has become so much part of your life. But there are other concerns.

Well, I am concerned about animals and how we treat them. I sometimes wonder if I have been too selfish in getting a puppy, because she didn't have much say in it.

Surprisingly, Lorelle, she did. Before she was born, she chose you as her parents, just as a human child chooses its parents. She knew she had to be a certain way to allow the breeder to select her for you, and this is what she has done.

Was there agreement between her and the breeder in spirit?

Not in the way that human souls arrange things, but yes, in a way.

Now she is where she always wanted to be. You also had a hand in choosing her, even though you were unaware of it. Your soul and her soul are linked.

Ok, but might not that be the case for a person and the one who they abuse in this life, in the way that the Friendly Soul volunteers to be a victim for someone?

Not in this case, Lorelle. But yes, that does happen.

You are right in your thinking that certain animal communicators would argue that animals do not volunteer to die or be abused at the hands of humans, and that is true on the level of consciousness on this planet, but on the level of soul consciousness, there is an agreement, which is hard for caring people to understand but without these agreements, there would be no lessons to learn on this planet. And there are many lessons to be learned here.

God, I am so grateful that there are cracks appearing in the live animal export industry, but I am sad that so many animals have had to suffer for us to get to this point. I want this to stop completely.

It will, Lorelle. The will of the people will prevail.

Is this also what is happening in the USA with the children separated from their parents (when President Trump ordered the separation of families at the border)?

Not really, Lorelle. It will be a while before sanity prevails in that country. As you know, even though Americans purport to worship God and follow the teachings of Jesus, most of them instead worship the dollars, and follow whichever teachings bring them more.

But they will get there in the end, just as you all will. Love will prevail in the end.

Yes, God.

Crime

Lorelle, I wanted to talk to you about crime.

Crime is on the increase in some areas, because people expect crime in those areas. It is time to focus only on the positive, on the reality that you desire, and crime will diminish.

Yes, God. Even our advertising media advertises crime, as a way to sell security screens, etc.

Yes, Lorelle. You know that there are other ways of securing your premises. You know that Archangel Michael is ready and waiting to install angels on every door and window in your house, and to keep a protective shield over your house and loved ones. Your intention of remaining safe and secure is important. If you expect to be safe and secure, this is what you will be.

Thank you, God.

❄❄❄

Sharing Love

Lorelle, I wanted to talk to you about love. You know that you fell in love with your new puppy straight away, and yet you feel that love at first sight among humans is a strange thing.

I guess we guard our love with humans, God. Not so, with animals.

That's right, Lorelle. You open your hearts to animals, and love comes instantly.

Is it that we just reflect back the love we are given?

No, Lorelle. You are open to give and receive love with animals. With humans, you close your hearts, or at least you believe you do, and that is why you experience that. In fact, you cannot close your hearts, but your powerful creative minds can believe that you can shield them from giving and receiving love.

Why is that?

Your society has rules about when and where you can give and receive love and you conform to them. These laws have been handed down across generations from your religions.

In a natural state, love would flow as freely between individual humans, as it does between human and animal. Can you imagine a world where love flowed so freely?

It is difficult for me to imagine. I have never seen it. I guess the free love era of the sixties was the closest, but perhaps that only happened with the aid of drugs, and I'm not sure that love flowed as freely as the sex did.

No, Lorelle, you are right. There has never been the free flow of love among all humans. There have been some groups in which love has flowed more freely than it does now, but never to all humans. It has generally been a case of them and us—love given selectively to us, but not to them.

Lorelle, you are coming into an era now, when love can flow freely between all humans, just as easily as it does between you and your pets. All it takes is the intention to create such a society.

But God, even other pets are not loved as much as our own. Is that purely intention?

That, too, is based on your beliefs that you can only love those in your own family. This is just part of your conditioning too, Lorelle.

Love can be freely shared with all. You have the capability if you will allow it and that is your natural state.

What would be the benefit of such a society? I am guessing that there would be some who would argue against it.

Yes, Lorelle, you could find people to argue against a society of free love, because free love is seen as sex without love, which is not what we are talking about. We are talking about a world where love is shared from the heart, and only from the genitals if and when appropriate.

Love is freely given and received when you allow your naturally open hearts to love as they were intended. You are love, and sharing love is your natural state. Just as you feel the love of trees when you walk through a forest, you would feel love emanating from every human as you walk through a crowd.

Are there any negatives to this kind of society?

No, Lorelle. The only negatives are those that you created with your negative thoughts. Love can never be negative, or it is not really love. Love is always positive and sharing more love will always have a positive result.

So, how can we achieve such a society, where love flows between every person on the planet?

You have to follow Jesus' advice to love your neighbour as yourself. Loving yourself is the necessary first step in loving your neighbour because until you can feel your own love, you cannot share it.

And how do we love our neighbour? Do we have to love ourselves first?

Not always, Lorelle, but it is a good first step, because if you can't love yourself, you will find it hard to love another fully.

You need to let go of judgment of yourself and others. Judgment is based on your ego's perspective, and your ego will always find fault with everyone, including yourself.

A person, including yourself, doesn't need to be faultless in order to be loved. In the eyes of God, there are no faults. In the eyes of God, you have all been created perfectly, and you are all doing the best you can in the situation in which you find yourselves.

You are love, and you are loved.

❄❄❄

Procreation

Now, Lorelle, we were talking about love. You know that is my favourite subject, and yours, too, if you recall from our previous conversations.

Yes, God.

We discussed how love is overtaking the planet, and how you can help to bring about this snowball of love, when we spoke during your book dictation, but now we want to talk about the process of making that happen.

You know that you have gone through a process to bring love to the forefront of your life. You uncovered your shadows, and you embraced your love. You acknowledged that you still have a way to go before you can be fully loving, but you are getting there. We spoke about how you need to avoid violence in all its forms, and you aim to do that as much as you can.

Now, the other things you found which helped you were to think love regularly, to live in the present moment, and to send love out into the world, because you know that it is returned to you tenfold. These are all wonderful ways of bringing love to yourself and the world.

We also spoke about sex, and the fact that sex is always love, even though in certain cases love isn't experienced during sex. But when love is experienced during sex, and when you use that time to also send love out into the world, your love is compounded, and that compounded love goes out into the world. So, as you make passionate love while sending love out into the world, you are saving the planet.

Now that we have gone over what we already know, I wanted to tell you some things that you may not be aware of. For instance, that, when you make love—that is have passionate love-making sex—you are also creating. You have heard of sex as a means of procreation. Do you know the literal meaning of procreation?

No. I'll look it up.

"To bring forth offspring"

"(From the Latin) *pro* = forth, *creare* = create"

That is right, Lorelle. You read in A Course in Miracles[12] *that your aim in life is to extend the love of God out into the universe. This is what you are doing when you are having sex—procreating—extending your love to the one you are with. And when you send your love out into the world at the same time, you are procreating even more, because you are sending your love out into the world—multiplying it tenfold.*

Sex is a wonderful thing for those involved in it, and for the planet and the universe. God is pleased by sex, Lorelle. God created humans to be creative beings. God created humans to procreate.

Many of your religions tell you that God is against sex in one form or another. But think about it. How could this be?

God has provided you with the physical, mental, and spiritual requirements to have loving, joyful sex. Why would God have provided you with such a means to joy, if she did not want you to use them?

Many would argue that God only wants sex to be used in procreation—that is the traditional meaning of the word.

Yes, Lorelle, and that was a great idea when the world needed more people to keep it operating efficiently. But now, as we discussed before, people really have no need to have large families, as they are unlikely to die young, and will be around to see their parents are looked after in their old age.

It is now no longer necessary to replace yourselves with offspring, as there are seven billion other people who can do that.

The procreation you can do during sex can send your love

out into the world. You can create forth your love, just as I have done in creating you. The love you send forth doesn't create more humans out there. It creates a more loving human within. As you procreate your love into the world, it returns to you tenfold, causing you to be more love than you were when you started. Your offspring is not in the form of human children, but in the form of human love, which really is God love, as all love is God love, as my love is dispersed amongst my creation.

Our love is all that is needed to save the world, Lorelle—your love and my love. You know that we are one, and you know that we are one with the rest of humanity, and the rest of creation. Your procreation affects all of my creation. You are creating forth, just as I have done.

It is harder for you to see the results of your creation, but when this life is finished, you will see just what you have created in all its glorious detail. You will be overjoyed at what you have achieved.

This will be what has been referred to as judgment day. This is not the day when God judges you as good or bad, and condemns you to eternal hell or allows you to eternal heaven. Judgment day is merely when you get to see the consequences of all your thoughts, words and deeds. You get to see the consequences for both yourself and others, directly and indirectly, and what might have happened if you had done things differently.

Might we feel guilty when we see that we have hurt ourselves or others by our actions?

There is no guilt in the afterlife, and no punishment. Yes, there are consequences, and those consequences have consequences. But there is no judgment, and there is no punishment.

Lorelle, we here on this side of the veil—the angels, your spirit guides, and all of your spiritual helpers—we all wish the best for you all and your planet. That is why we are trying hard now to bring more love to your planet—to allow there to be a critical mass when love will create a snowball effect that will overtake the world. You are not there yet, but you are not far off.

I know you see the events of the world, like children being locked up and separated from their parents, like animals being inhumanely treated, and you wonder how far you have to go to reach a world where love rules the planet. Trust me when I tell you that love does rule the planet now. Most people aren't aware of it.

There is no right or wrong. There is only that which brings you closer to or further away from your goals of a world where everyone is treated with respect, including Mother Earth.

All that has been happening on your planet has allowed many more people to wake up to the reality that their goal in life is not money or more of what it can buy, but more love. And when people wake up to what their real goals are, they start actively trying to bring that into being. Lorelle, more and more people are acting to bring about a world filled with love.

If you can be love, think love, and act with love, you will bring more love into the world. If you send your love out into the world, you will bring more love into the world. If you have sex while sending your love out into the world, you will bring more love into the world.

❊ ❊ ❊

You Were Created Perfectly

Hello, Lorelle. What would you like to talk about this evening?

Whatever you like, God.

I like you, Lorelle, so we could talk about you.

We could.

You don't seem too keen.

No.

Why is that?

Not sure.

Lorelle, it is because you know that I know all about you, that there is nothing that you can hide from me. You fear that knowledge will lead to criticism or worse, being unloved. But you know that I created you, and I love everything about you, even those things you perceive as flaws. In fact, they are not flaws, but special traits. They are what make you special. Flaws, as you perceive them, in your personality are either designed aspects of your personality necessary to achieve your aims in this life, or aspects designed to allow you to learn lessons in relation to them.

Every human on the planet was perfectly created, and is

perfect in every way, now and eternally. There is nothing that you can do that can create flaws in my creation. You are all perfect.

So, Lorelle, can we talk about you now?

Oh, I thought that was us talking about me.

No. We need to get a bit more personal.

Ok.

Lorelle, you know that there are aspects of your personality that you would like to change, if given a chance. You know that you become angry sometimes, and regret that, when you take that anger out on unsuspecting people. You know that you are a little obsessive and react badly when everything is not 'just so'. You also know that living with a husband who is not so worried about tidiness has allowed you to mellow somewhat.

Yes. I had to mellow or blow a fuse. Still, I react when enough buttons are pushed.

Yes, Lorelle, you do. You know that that button-pushing is designed to bring those things to your attention, so that you can change if you so desire. Everything in your life is designed perfectly to create the result that you desire, and to allow you opportunities for growth.

If you can look at your life from a different perspective, you will appreciate all that has happened and is happening in your life. You may not have the opportunity to see everything from that alternative perspective during your lifetime, but afterwards, as we discussed previously, you have the opportunity to know the consequences of everything you think, say, and do, but also to look at everything from other perspectives, so that you can fully understand and appreciate all that has occurred in your life.

A Different Perspective on Health Issues

Would you like to look at some of the events in your life from a different perspective now?

If you like.

I know you are thinking about your craziness, Lorelle, but you already have seen a slightly different perspective of that, as you have been led to carry out research into psychotic episodes, their causes and treatments.

Ok.

Lorelle, you know that you have had a couple of long-term health issues—your thyroid issue for example.
You know that many people have had their thyroids removed after suffering from more malignant forms of your goitre, but most people who have a similar condition to yours have been told that they need to take drugs for the rest of their lives, as you were.

You were lucky enough to see a doctor who drew your attention to the link between your condition and iodine, so you have been able to stabilise your condition to a certain extent, by supplementing your iodine intake.

You also know stress has played a large part in the formation and ongoing maintenance of your goitre. You have felt it respond to stress. You have not, however, felt the benefits occurring every time you meditate. Your meditation has a reversing effect to the effects of stress. Unfortunately, your society and your planet create so much stress that you have not fully reversed the effects of stress, but you will.

Even if your higher self has reasons for creating your health issues—to bring you a lesson or a higher outcome of which you may not be aware—you can always ask for help. Firstly, you can meditate to find out the wishes of your higher self. Once you know the aims of the health issue, even if you don't know how to achieve those aims, you can ask for help to achieve those aims. Once those aims are achieved, you may be able to release that health issue.

❋ ❋ ❋

What God Is Not

Hello, Lorelle. What would you like to talk about this evening?

Last night we talked about me. Tonight, we should talk about you.

Ok, Lorelle. What did you want to know?

Whatever you would like to tell me.

I would like to tell you what I am not, Lorelle.
I am not a judgmental God. I am not vengeful. I am not a God of wrath, as you learned about in the Old Testament.

Are you the same God who created us all? The same God who existed in the days of the Old Testament?

Yes and no, Lorelle. Yes, I am the same God, but no, I'm not the same as existed then.
God created the universe out of God. The physical universe is forever changing, so God is forever changing. Yet, I am unchanging, in that I am forever love. Ultimate Reality, as we discussed previously, is what I am, and Ultimate Reality is unchanging, unconditional love. However, as God appears in time and space, God is all things, including judgmental, vengeful, and wrathful.

So, if we are aiming to be Godlike, should we aim to be like Ultimate Reality, or like the judgmental, vengeful, wrathful God?

You know I will not tell you what you should do, but depending on your aims in life, you should focus upon being that which brings you closer to them. From what I understand, your aims are to have a world where everyone is treated with respect, where love rules and peace reigns. If these are your aims, it would serve you best to aim to be most like Ultimate Reality, which is unconditional love.

Has God evolved from the God of wrath of the Old Testament to the God of love today, or have you always been the God of love, but people misunderstood you?

I have always been the God of love, Lorelle. There has been some misunderstanding, but a lot of the things you think of as being enacted by a God of wrath, were enacted by a God of love, because some of the story has been left out or distorted.

Everything on this planet and in this universe is made of love, and everything that happens on this planet and in this universe is caused by love.

❊ ❊ ❊

God Is Unconditional Love

Lorelle, what would you like to talk about?

Our conversation ended rather abruptly last night. Had you finished telling me about yourself?

Well, Lorelle, I told you what I'm not, and I told you about time and space and Ultimate Reality. What I didn't tell you too much about was the love that I am. I am a love that you can only dream of, but even in your dreams you cannot experience its full extent. You experienced a large dose of my love when we were writing your previous books, and you even dipped into the well of ecstasy of my love, but even then, you didn't experience the full extent of my love.

My love creates worlds and all who dwell on them.

If your love creates worlds and all who dwell on them, why do we have unloving beings? I know you said that from a broader perspective every action is one of love, even if it is just love of self.

If we are all created from your unconditional love, why do we not all experience and act with unconditional love?

Lorelle, in order to experience heat, you must understand cold; to understand down, you have to understand up. I created a universe of duality where you could experience a full spectrum of love, so that when you experience love higher up the spectrum, you recognise it as such.

Life is filled with many rich experiences, made possible by this world of duality.

Did I get that wrong, that it is this world where duality exists, or is it the universe?

There is more than one universe, Lorelle, but this universe is a universe of duality, at least the part of it that you are aware of. There is far more to life and my creation than you can understand.

Suffice to say that everything is perfect, just as it should be, and everything is love.

If you are not experiencing everything as love, it is because you are looking at it from the wrong perspective. Not that there is a right and wrong, except if you want to look at something from the perspective of all love, then the perspective where it isn't all love is wrong, if that is your aim.

Do you understand?

I understand what you have said, but I don't understand how to tell someone who is suffering at the hands of another that the act that is causing their suffering is a loving act, and they just have to change their point of view.

Perhaps in hindsight, that perspective may be possible, but while they are suffering, they are not likely to have that ability.

No, Lorelle, you are right. But it is not necessary to suffer if you do not wish to. You know that you get to choose how much suffering you experience. No one needs to suffer if they don't wish to. The experiences any being has in life are dictated by their soul. If your soul doesn't wish you to suffer, you can ask now for no more suffering, and that would be the result.

How can we know if our soul wants us to suffer?

By asking, Lorelle. Ask and you shall receive. You and your soul are one being, but you are not always aware of your soul's aims in this life. However, if you ask during meditation, you will know the answer.

Is it possible that one's soul would answer incorrectly, if its aims dictate for us not to know?

It is possible but unlikely. You and your soul are one, and your desires are one. If you desire no more suffering, your soul is likely to as well.

❄❄❄

Life

Life isn't what most of you think it is. It is not merely the time you spend in your physical form between your physical birth and death. Life is what I am, and what you are. Life is All That Is. Life for us humans is only the physical part of an eternal life that you cannot even imagine. Life for All That Is exists in all of my creation. Life exists in those things that you might have previously thought of as lifeless, such as rocks and grains of sand. I am in everything, and therefore life is in everything.

God, I can sort of accept that life is in everything that you have created, but is life in plastics, glass and bricks, and things that humans have made?

Yes, Lorelle, not as elemental as in the original creation, but life is there in all things. There is no conscious being in most of these things, but usually your planet speaks on behalf of all of those less conscious beings, such as rocks and grains of sand. She is not so able to speak on behalf of those things that humans have made, but she is still their mother, even though humans may be their father, so to speak.

Don't worry, Lorelle; life on this planet is here to stay. You love your planet and all who dwell on her but you have not yet attained unconditional love for All That Is. You still have trouble cuddling a cockroach or a crocodile, and you are not too keen on some humans, but you love your mother, the Earth, and wish her to prosper. All who dwell on her would prosper, too, if you allowed the Earth to prosper, and allowed her to see that all who depend on her prosper too. You know that she wants only the best for all of her children.

God, how can we know what is best for Mother Earth and All That Is?

You can know when you remember to listen to your internal guidance and follow your feelings. Your feelings are the voice of your soul, but you also have angels and guides to help you as well as my counsel, if you listen.

When you listen to a different voice—the voice of your ego—you hear the voice of fear. Your ego tells you that you must compete for resources, and that there is not enough for everyone. You take from others and hoard for a rainy day. You don't trust the universe to provide for you, so you think you have to take what you can get now.

The ideal situation would be where you shared your resources and understood that there is enough for all. When you understand there is enough, and you trust the universe to provide for your future, you have no need to hoard.

❄︎❄︎❄︎

War

Lorelle, I wanted to talk, not about love, but about war.

You know that there are many different types of war waged on your planet. People declare war often—war on want, war on terror, war between countries, between religions, between tribes. Do you know what all of these have in common?

No.

They are all forms of expression of love.

I know you find it hard to believe. But it is true. Each of these groups which declare war on something or someone do it out of love, or what they think is love, at least, even if it is only love of self.

"So, if love is the basis of war, how can we put an end to war?" you may well ask.

Well, love is often expressed in ways that do not support the aims people say they have. The way to end war is to clarify your aim.

Can we take an example, God, so that it is easier to understand?

Yes, Lorelle.

What about war on terror?

Ok, Lorelle. I am guessing that the aim of declaring war on terror is to reduce the number of terror attacks in those countries declaring war. The problem with this is that, by declaring war, it is just alienating more people, and alienating those already alienated even more.

The key word here is 'alienate'.

When we think in terms of us and them, and declare war on them, we make them the aliens. We are thus creating greater separation between us and them.

Instead, in order to achieve the stated aims of reducing terror attacks, it is necessary to reduce the separation rather than increase it.

And how do we do that?

You know the answer already, Lorelle—more love. But rather than only loving us, we also have to love them, and this is hard for people to do.

In your book by the Dalai Lama[13], you learned how to offer compassion and prayers for happiness to your friends, then strangers, then enemies. You learned to reduce the separation between us and them.

Rather than just loving those we see as us, we need to share our love with those we see as them as well. We need to start dialogue with them, finding as much common ground as possible. We need to start seeing every person, every being, as one of us.

The saying: "There but for the grace of God" is helpful in this. It allows you to realise that, given different circumstances, you could have ended up in the position that others who are considered to be 'them' are in.

With dialogue, you can allow them to share their joys and their troubles, while you do the same with them. The first step is always more love. In fact, every step involves more love—love for all and this applies to all of the wars we discussed.

What about war on want?

The Bible says: "The Lord is my shepherd. I shall not want." There is no separation between you and the rest of the universe which supplies all of your needs. There is no need to want.

The idea of a war on want comes from the idea that there is a lack of resources on your planet, so the war is against lack. However, there is no lack, and there are resources enough for all. Some people have more of one resource and less of another. It should be possible to share your resources fairly, without any need to declare war.

We are all one. Every war is caused by the belief in separation between us.

Love is the answer to all questions. Every person on the planet has an internal guidance system designed to allow each person to fairly share their resources with love for self and All That Is.

❄︎❄︎❄︎

Love Is the Answer

We spoke before that every act of war is really an act of love, whether love of self or country or tribe, etc., but you know that you are trying to create a world where peace reigns, and love rules, so you want to find a way to reduce acts of war and increase acts of love. The key is to think love more often. Love is what you are, so thinking love is easy for you, even though you are mostly out of practice.

Lorelle, you and the other humans on your planet would like to create a peaceful world but have forgotten how to do that. Admittedly, there have been times when it has been necessary for people to declare war in order to achieve peace, but those times in history have been very rare.

The answer to every question is love so if the question is whether or not we should declare war, the answer is to throw some love at the situation first. If love fails when love is tried from every possible angle, then war may be necessary, but only in order to stop someone else from hurting others. Yet those who are being hurt can help too, by loving the offending person or nation. Love overrides anything, so if enough love is delivered to a situation or a problem, a solution will appear.

God, I have found with Tiki (our puppy), when she is playing too rough, it is difficult to give love when I am being hurt.

And yet you do, Lorelle, without realising it. It has become an automatic response for you, even while you are getting angry and trying other means to overcome her behaviour. Love is emitted from you. You also don't realise that it is having an effect—slow and steady—in getting Tiki to change her ways.

How can others learn this, God?

Just as you did, Lorelle. Ask and you shall receive. You know that you did not always like the lessons you faced but they allowed you to practise thinking love in difficult situations. You can always ask for easier lessons.

Lorelle, you and all of my creation are a delight to me. I am more delighted when I can have a conversation with you and others who wish to, and even more so when I can share my love with you all, as I have with you in the past.

❄❄❄

The Lion Lies down with the Lamb

God, I wanted to talk to you about a couple of things that caused me questions from our previous talks.

Ok, Lorelle.

The first was when you talked about love flowing freely between all humans being our natural state.

Yes, Lorelle.

You said that where we have saved our love for only our family and don't share it with everyone, it is because of our society's laws. Then I thought of animals. They have family groups, with which they share their love, and withhold their love from others.

Yes, they have societies much like your own. Was that not written in the Qur'an that animals have communities similar to humans?

Human thoughts on this planet control love more than it would be in its natural state, even amongst animals considered to be wild. Humans don't understand their power. When all humans can share their love with each other and All That Is, the likelihood of all animals doing the same increases exponentially. It could truly be a time when the lion lies down with the lamb.

Until then, though, sending your love out into the world is helping.

Which God?

I was confused by our discussion about the God of wrath in time and space. You started the conversation by stating what you are not—that you are not judgmental, vengeful, or wrathful. Then later you said that in time and space, you are all these things.

I didn't understand this. Were you saying that the you that has been separated into parts of your creation can be judgemental? Or were you saying that God, the creator entity, can be all these things too, when you enter time and space?

Which do you think?

It doesn't matter what I think.

Yes, it does, Lorelle. In time and space, you co-create God. You, and the rest of my creation are God, in time and space.

So, that brings me back to my question, which Angela asked in my earlier books: "If God is made up of all of her creation in time and space, where are these conversations coming from then?"

I am All That Is, Lorelle, but, as I said before, I am greater than the sum of my parts, just as you are.

But when I talk to God, am I talking to the unconditionally loving God of Ultimate Reality, or the possibly judgmental, possibly wrathful God of time and space?

You are talking to yourself, Lorelle. You are talking to the God that you believe in, the one you have created with your thoughts. If you desire to talk to only the Ultimate Reality God, then that will be your experience. If you wish to talk to the God of time and space who can be judgmental, then that will be your experience.

I would always wish to speak to the God of Ultimate Reality. Can the God of Ultimate Reality still answer questions about experiences in time and space? Or are your answers then only limited to love?

Yes, Lorelle. Love is the answer to all questions, whether in time and space or in Ultimate Reality. And remember that all things are possible for God so God can be whatever you desire her to be. The God of Ultimate Reality is unchanging, but the God of time and space is all things to all people.

Did that answer your question?

Yes and no.

That's right, Lorelle. You are still confused because you will always have trouble comprehending God. God is so much more than you can ever imagine, and God is possible of being so much more than that as well. There is no way that you can understand God completely with your limited understanding and perspective.

Suffice to say that I am all love, but I am also all that you desire in a God. If you want God to be judgmental, I can be that.

What if I want God to smite my enemies, would you do that?

Not me, per se, Lorelle, but I have created a universe where you can have all of your desires, whilst everyone else has theirs as well, if you believe it so.

But what if my desire is not to be smitten, and my enemy's desire is to see me smitten?

Then, Lorelle, the universe has to find a way to achieve both of your desires. Because the universe listens to the energy of the desire, it is more swayed by a strong desire, if you believe it is possible.

This is why prayer and faith are very important in these situations.

Ok, thanks.

❋❋❋

Delegation

I wanted to talk to you about your book, but then I will let your angels finish it for you. You know that angels are my agents who act on my behalf for humans. You will be given information which has a divine source but will be given to you by the angels. Do you understand?

Yes, but I don't understand the reason for the differentiation.

Suffice to say that the angels are better able to communicate with you about these things because of their experience in communicating with humans.

Are you saying that God is less capable than his/her angels?

No, I am saying that God has learned to delegate, which is something that I'm sure you understand.

I do understand about delegation, but if God is

omnipresent and infinite, God has infinite capability of communicating with all creation.

Yes, you are right. So why do I need angels?

I don't know.

I don't need them, Lorelle. You do. You need the help of spiritual beings, of which angels are one type. My angels are your angels. Your angels are my angels. We are one. The angels carry some of my light and love and can distribute it around the universe for me, as they are assigned to do. There is a hierarchy with the archangels in charge of the angels which communicate and deal with life on your planet.

You have some experience with communicating with Michael, and a little with Gabriel and perhaps a couple of others briefly. You know that the angels' and archangels' roles change according to needs. Michael, for example, has been given more responsibility on the Earth as you move towards a new Earth and new spirituality on Earth. He is here now to help you all transition towards that new spirituality, which we spoke of in your last book. Michael is here now. Would you like to speak to him?

Yes, if that is your wish.

Yes, it is my wish that Michael helps you at this time. As you know, the angels who spoke to you previously did so as an anonymous conglomerate, because just as you humans are one, so too are the angels, but angels are aware of this. They can speak as one. Michael is differentiating himself from the other angels to give you humans a figurehead, a persona to speak and relate to in the current time of transition.

Traditionally it has been Gabriel who is seen as the messenger archangel, and he/she is still doing that role, but Michael has taken on an overarching role, looking after the health and safety of the whole planet, particularly humans, and steps forward now to communicate with you.

I want you to feel comfortable communicating with Michael, not only about your personal issues, but also about global issues. I want you all to feel confident in your abilities as children of God, and Michael is seen as boosting people's confidence in their ability to feel safe and secure in the world. He can also assist in healings, just as Raphael and Jesus have done. We would like Michael to be the one who is seen as the go-to-guy, as you might say in your vernacular.

Now, Lorelle, I will hand you over to Michael to carry on the conversation. You know that you can call on me at any time. I am with you always, but Michael will be available too, to help you as you transition.

❆❆❆

Messages from Archangel Michael

Overcoming the Pandemic

Hello, Lorelle. It is Archangel Michael here.

At this time, there are strange things happening on your planet, the COVID pandemic being the major one on everyone's minds. There is controversy about the origins of the virus, about the level of deaths compared to less serious illnesses, controversy over natural immunity versus inoculation of vaccines, and the loss of freedoms experienced as governments attempt to combat what they see as an enemy virus.

As those of you of spiritual training know, combat is not a good idea under any circumstances. Yes, sometimes wars are necessary, but is it necessary to declare war on a virus, particularly when the virus you declare war on today is not the same one which is attacking you tomorrow, after it mutates?

The answer to all questions is love. Just as Mother Teresa did not wish to march in a protest march against war, many spiritual people understand that fighting against something only brings it further into your consciousness, and makes it more real. For those of you who understand the law of attraction, you know that the more you fear something, the more you bring it into your consciousness. The more thoughts you have about it, the more thoughts you attract about it.

Vaccinations are a way for people to focus on the healthy solution to a problem, rather than the problem itself, so it brings healing as the thoughts of people turn away from fear towards safety and health. However, with every new wave of hysteria which begins with every new variant, the tide turns in the other direction.

What to do?

You need do nothing but think love towards everyone involved, including the virus. You have been told that viruses are not alive, and this may be true by some reckoning, but even so, you know that even crystals, which are seen as lumps of rock are alive in the spiritual sense, and respond to love, just as all of life does.

Thoughts of love toward the virus and all those affected by it, bring more thoughts of love, and love conquers all. I can help you and all humans end this pandemic, not with weapons or combat, but with love. If we think of ending a pandemic, which is the overbalancing of the equilibrium normally held between a virus and its hosts, it is not the same as eradicating the virus. We need to think only of eradicating the imbalance, which is the cause of the problem, not the virus.

You are a child of God. All humans are children of God, and therefore capable of becoming invincible to this virus and this pandemic, but first you need to stop attracting it with every thought and word. It is time to focus on love. I can help you with this.

Why not start a prayer vigil to pray for peace—peace from the fear of an intangible virus, something which cannot be seen by a human eye.

Humans have been combating the common cold and influenza for centuries. Has that eradicated those viruses from your planet?

Love will bring back the equilibrium. Balance is what is required. Love is the answer.

❋❋❋

Moving forward into the New Spirituality

We are here to discuss the way you and your fellow humans can best move forward into the New Spirituality. As we mentioned, it is time now to forget about COVID. You can still take precautions and follow health advice, but without putting any thought into propagating fear, as has happened previously.

Even though it might be a new virus with perhaps greater consequences, just think of it as a flu and the precautions you take to stop getting flu. You can take the extra precautions recommended for COVID, without becoming fearful and filled with dread. You can also take those precautions that your health authorities perhaps aren't proposing, like eating a healthy diet, with adequate fruit and vegetable intake. You can reduce your intake of animal products, processed foods, and chemicals including from smoking. Instead, increase those things which improve immunity and help to make your body more adept at fighting off viruses. Your body has developed a wonderful system of detecting and dealing with viruses, even those it has never seen before. You all have wonderful bodies, capable of great adaptation. Just as viruses adapt, so too do human bodies.

You really have nothing to fear from this virus if you remember to honour your body and mind and keep them in tip-top condition. Although diseases and viruses can affect your body, your mind has the greatest effect. Why is it that some people never get a cold, and some people get every cold going around? Your faith in your body to maintain health in the face of viral or other infection is most powerful.

As I said, I am not suggesting for you not to follow health directives. I am, in fact, suggesting that you remain even more vigilant, by having the healthiest body you can, before coming into contact with the virus. But if you do come in contact with the virus, have faith in your body's abilities. Have faith in your spiritual helpers to get you the best care appropriate for your condition, and have faith in your creator, who created you as a child of God with all of God's attributes.

I know that many of you think that God only created one Son, but did not Jesus tell you that you are his brothers and sisters? God has given you everything you need to get by in this world, in this life and the greatest of the resources he has given you is love.

Faith is also required. This is something you are born with, but which you generally lose during your life. Does not a newborn babe have faith that its needs will be met? It cries and knows that it will be fed and clothed and loved. It is only as a babe grows that it learns from its parents that there are now things which are withheld at some times in some circumstances. Prior to these lessons from its parents and society, it is confident of being cared for, confident that God has provided a means for it to survive and thrive.

And remember from your book, Getting Used to Weird[14]*, when Angela discussed with God the fact that no one dies against their will. Every soul has a choice about the time and nature of its physical death. Sometimes the physical human is unaware, but you are always aware on a soul level and your death is not set in concrete; you have choices.*

Often you make arrangements with other souls in order for them to have certain experiences in their lives, so people want to honour those arrangements, even though their physical personality may not think it is the best course of action.

You are a three-part being—body, mind and soul. Your soul is in charge, but nothing happens against its will. If you meditate regularly, you are more likely to always be aware of your soul's wishes. But as I said, nothing is written in stone. Circumstances can change.

The best way for humans to move forward into the New Spirituality is to stay in close contact with your higher selves, to communicate with your spiritual helpers, as you have learned to do, and to have faith.

But the greatest lesson is the lesson of love. Take love with you wherever you go, and you are invincible. Share your love with others and you help them become invincible too. Be at peace, knowing you have all of the resources you need to move forward towards the New Spirituality

Remember, we are all one. You are one with all of God's creation, including all humans. Rather than endeavouring to separate yourself from others, it is important to remember your unity, as this will help you move forward together towards the New Spirituality. Yes, take precautions, but don't isolate yourself. Even if it is necessary to isolate yourself physically, keep in touch with each other electronically or by phone.

Look out for your neighbours and friends. Everyone has love within them, but everyone needs love, particularly in times of stress. You can send your love out into the world so that it reaches everyone on the planet. You can also share your love with those close to you, even if it is just waving to someone over the fence. Hug as many people as you can, as physical touch is a great healer. If you can't get physical, your intention to send them love is nearly as good.

Don't worry about where we will go from here. You will receive sufficient information to proceed towards your goals, towards a world where love rules, and everyone, including all the animals and Mother Earth, are all treated with respect.

Now go forth into the world. Follow directives regarding health precautions and honour your bodies with the best that you can give them. Remember to love yourself first and then you have love to share with others. Have faith in yourself and your creator. Call upon your spiritual helpers for help. I am here to help you, so call on me to help with your confidence and faith, and to help keep you safe and healthy.

We are one, so we all want this to work. We all desire a world where the New Spirituality comes into being with the least amount of pain and suffering along the way.

Love is the answer to all questions. Make love the dominant force in your life and we are all sure to succeed.

❈❈❈

Living With COVID

We are not yet at the stage where we can tell you to forget about COVID completely, because people are still contracting the virus and some are still dying from it in the physical sense. You know that you are eternal beings and it is only the death of your physical body we are talking about.

As we mentioned, your spiritual being is eternal. Your essence is eternal, so there is nothing to fear from a virus, because it can't kill your true, spiritual self. But if you wish to preserve your physical body as long as possible, it is necessary to follow the directions of your health advisors, and follow our advice regarding improving your immunity.

There has been much discussion about natural immunity versus immunity from vaccination, but people can have both. We have asked you to reduce the amount of chemicals you put into your body, but we are confident that you, as children of God, can help your bodies to survive the impact the chemicals in the vaccinations will have on them and still thrive, if you believe it so. As we mentioned, your attitude to this is important. Keep a positive outlook about the effects of the vaccinations and the effects of the virus. You can withstand many things if you believe it so.

Remember that Jesus performed many miracles: healing the sick and bringing others back to life after their perceived death. He also reappeared after his own physical death.

I am not saying that you are all sufficiently spiritually developed to be able to withstand a crucifixion and come back to life afterwards, although you could, given sufficient faith.

What I am saying is that you are stronger than you think. You are more powerful than you think, and your power can be made manifest in a healthy body, regardless of what goes into it. Even though I asked you to reduce your chemical intake, it may be preferable to intake chemicals in a vaccination which may also have a positive effect on your body's ability to withstand the effects of the virus, rather than intake chemicals which are of no benefit whatsoever.

Is there anything you would like to ask me, Lorelle?

Yes. If we are afraid that the vaccines might have nasty side effects, might that fear be enough to attract those side effects to us?

It is possible, Lorelle, but don't forget that your higher self has complete control over what happens to you. So if you are afraid of the effects of the vaccine, ask during meditation if there are likely to be any side effects and you can then be prepared and make a considered decision about what course to take.

What about what God was saying that it is sometimes not in our higher self's best interests for us to be consciously aware of what might happen. Might we not be misled by our higher selves?

Your higher self will never mislead you. You may not receive an answer, but you will never be lied to by your higher self. Your ego self, on the other hand, often lies to you, particularly about risks to itself, which are often associated in your ego mind with risks to your physical body. If you allowed your ego complete control over all your actions, you would never take any actions, because your ego would talk you out of doing anything because of fear.

Fear can sometimes keep your body alive—for instance stopping you from going too close to a cliff edge—but your ego is also kept alive by fear. This is why it likes to keep you in fear, so it doesn't risk its existence. If you decided there was nothing to fear in life, you wouldn't need your ego. You would simply listen to your higher self, which would tell you that there is nothing to fear in this world or the next. You are a child of God, an invincible being. If you could believe that every minute of every day, you would know that you have nothing to fear, and you would never listen to your ego voice again.

As you learned from God, your ego has its place, but it is meant to be subservient to your higher self, not the other way around. Even if you keep a balance between your higher self and ego self, you can lead a productive life, making a positive impact on the world, as you succeed in achieving your aims you came into this life to achieve. When you listen only to your ego's voice, you live in fear, and are made immobile, too frightened to move. You are never likely to achieve much if you listen only to your ego voice.

As we mentioned, fear is not a bad thing; it can keep your body safe. But you don't want to listen to your ego voice, which would keep you paralysed from fear.

You know the answer is to think love often. Love is the answer to all questions and love can overcome fear. I know that you had many lessons about love, which you wrote about in

Getting Used to Weird. *If you only knew that we are all made of love and that love is all around us, you would never fear love again.*

You are love; I am love; everything is love. It is love which can make sure that you listen to your higher self and don't allow your ego voice to keep you in fear.

Go now and take love with you wherever you go. In fact, you can't help but take love with you wherever you go, because you are love. But if you consciously take love with you wherever you go by thinking love often, you will know there is nothing to fear.

❄❄❄

Messages from God

Masculine Michael

(I had not felt completely comfortable talking to Michael. Although I hadn't previously had long discussions with Michael, I had felt his energy often, as I call on him to help remove negative and foreign energy from my energy field as part of my preparation for doing my daily card readings. The energy I had felt previously still filled me with joy, as the majority of angel conversations had done, except when the subject matter troubled me.)

God, I am concerned that I didn't feel joy when talking to Michael. Something's wrong here. I don't know what it is, but I don't think I can carry on talking to Michael until I find out.

Lorelle, it is just that he has a different energy than you are used to. You know that you have recently had brought to your attention the Feminine Archangel books. This is no coincidence. The angels you have spoken to previously are truly genderless—being neither masculine nor feminine. Michael is like all other angels and archangels—without gender, as I am. But, in order to carry out his role on Earth, he takes on a masculine energy.

For you it feels even more masculine because your energy is very feminine. He is still a being of love. He still projects love everywhere he looks and onto everything he touches, but it appears as masculine love to your sensitive sensors.

You can have faith that you are talking to a being of light and love, who is indeed helping all of your planet move towards the New Spirituality.

Don't worry. You can ask him to present a more pleasing energy for you if you wish. Would that make you feel better?

I guess, but is there a reason for him presenting himself to me in his more masculine form, in a form that caused me discomfort?

No, Lorelle. I know you have learned that everything happens for a reason, but the only reason for him presenting himself as he did was so that we could discuss gender in angels and archangels. It might be timely for you to read one of the books that you saw about feminine archangels, and we can discuss it afterwards.

God, I know Michael is unlikely to be offended, but I feel guilty for feeling the way I did.

Think nothing of it. Michael knows that this conversation was on the cards, so to speak. He realises the reasons for your feelings and, as you say, he will not be so easily offended.

I do feel a bit like Truman in *The Truman Show* again, as I did on occasion previously, where it seems that my version of reality is being manipulated and where everyone else knows what is going on but me.

I know, Lorelle, but it is all in a good cause, and you enjoy the fun and adventure.

Patriarchal Society

We said we will discuss the feminine archangels when you have read the book, but I wanted to start the conversation now, if that's ok. You have spoken to a few archangels, and they have helped you with certain issues in your life. There are many archangels you haven't met that you know of, but others still whom you have not heard of.

As I started to tell you last night about Archangel Michael, other archangels whom you have met have been more masculine than feminine for the most part, such as Raphael. Some, like Gabriel, are seen as both masculine and feminine. We now wish you to get used to associating a number of archangels with their feminine identities, and we will be introducing you to a few archangels you have not yet met.

We have had a long period of history on this planet, when the masculine has reigned supreme, especially as a result of the patriarchy of religions. However, it has been a bit of a chicken and egg situation where the patriarchy has caused the emphasis on the masculine, and the emphasis on the masculine has reinforced the patriarchy.

In many nations on the planet now, the female humans are being given more emphasis in governments and corporate hierarchies. But often those organisations have been run along masculine guidelines. When men make the rules and create the structures which create the rules, females often need to emphasise their masculine attributes to succeed. You know that males and female humans have both masculine and feminine attributes. Masculine attributes are encouraged in men, while female attributes are discouraged. Feminine attributes are not honoured as much as masculine attributes, ever since the witch trials, which demonised women who were outspoken or who practised herbal cures, or just for being women who looked different or acted differently.

There is a long history of dominance by the masculine on this planet, and even now, when women are more emancipated, they still bear scars in their psyche of being subordinate to men and being victimised by a patriarchal society or religion.

It took years to get to this far, and any movement to get a better balance between masculine and feminine will be a slow process. We don't want the balance to tip in the other direction, and we don't want it to tip back towards the masculine, so we need to take one step at a time.

Everyone can play their part by honouring the feminine aspects in both men and women—allowing boys to cry, respecting intuition and psychic development, listening to and honouring emotions as well as intellect.

We are doing our bit on the spiritual side by introducing you all to more feminine angels and archangels.

❈❈❈

Gender Change

We were talking about why you heard and felt Archangel Michael differently when you spoke to him, and we mentioned that it was because he was purposely giving you a masculine impression of himself, even more so than usual. Because of his role, he is usually portrayed and perceived as masculine, but you know that, as with all spiritual beings, they are neither masculine nor feminine.

I know you were just thinking about the tendency in modern times for children not to be defined as masculine or feminine until they decide which they wish to be. You know that many would like to see this tendency stopped, because, in their eyes, their gender is decided by their genetic and physical makeup, not by their spiritual choices. Humans, however, are spiritual beings having a physical experience, so, in fact, they could change their mind about their gender once incarnated, but it would be a rare occurrence. Most people who incarnate have already chosen their gender and their sexuality before incarnating, but there is nothing to stop a being from changing midstream, so to speak.

You know that physical laws on your planet can be overcome with miracles, which are just the use of your God-given powers of love plus faith. However, at this time in your development, it would be rare for a human to have sufficient faith to be able to change their physical makeup without some sort of intervention by drugs or surgery. We do not wish to comment on the morality of such actions, because, as you know, God does not have an opinion one way or the other, only to offer advice on which path would serve people best, given what they are trying to accomplish in life.

Although we in spirit know what individual humans are trying to accomplish in their lives, you, as humans are not generally given this knowledge about others. We would therefore suggest that it is not in your best interests to judge those actions as right or wrong, because you cannot know what is right or wrong for another being. So, as long as it is not harming another being, it is not in your best interests to interfere.

Female Archangels

As you know, you have just been reading the book by Claire Stone about The Female Archangels[15]*, which she called Archeiai. What did you think of the book, Lorelle?*

I found it interesting, but I didn't feel a strong urge to connect with any particular archaiai, although I would like to if I am able and have the time. Was there something I was particularly meant to take away from the book?

No, Lorelle. It was just a way to bring up the subject of spiritual gender. You have always known that angels and archangels are without gender but show themselves to humans in the form best suited to their role and the message they would like to convey. Michael is often perceived as masculine, and Gabriel is seen often as feminine, but both are neither masculine nor feminine, but without gender.

They are not, as you might think, the same as humans which are a mixture of masculine and feminine but with a stronger leaning towards one gender or another. You know that sometimes homosexual humans seem to be closer to the middle of the separation between male and female, but still identify as one gender or another.

All humans are born with some masculine and some feminine traits. As you learned in genetics in your biology class, the conception of humans comes about when a sperm and an egg combine and the chromosomes in the zygote create a being with either xx or xy sex chromosomes, which determine the gender of the child.

I am sorry, God, I am trying to remember my lessons, but can't.

I know, Lorelle. You know you have trouble thinking of other things when taking dictation, because you have learned to close off your ego mind to a certain extent.

Anyway, the child who is born as either a male or female still has some attributes from the other gender. All humans have some testosterone and some oestrogen in their bodies, which determine their leanings towards masculine or feminine traits.

Angels and archangels, however, have no such hormones running through their systems. Their appearance as male or female is entirely for the benefit of their audience. The archaiai were indeed archangels which were more present on the Earth during a time when the feminine aspects in humans were considered more noteworthy and prior to the Earth being overtaken by patriarchal systems.

As was mentioned in the book about archaiai, it is now time in Earth's history to bring back a balance between male and female influence. The balance may need to go in the other direction for a while until an equilibrium is reached, just as scales do.

The archaiai are showing themselves more now, to help bring about these shifts in the balance of influence on Earth. Rather than being male or female, it is their roles which require them to be perceived as more feminine than the previous more masculine archangels.

❊❊❊

Gender in Relationships

Lorelle, last night you asked whether in the process of becoming one on your planet, you need to remove the separation between genders. And the answer is yes and no. Yes, in the spiritual sense, but no in the physical sense.

Part of the fun of incarnating on Earth is the pleasure of learning about Life, which is another name for God, through relationships: to learn about love, life and God in a relationship of male and female. I know that special relationships are possible between two males and two females, but the relationship between male and female creates a more complete whole when combined. It is harder for a same sex couple to create balance, harder but not impossible. Having said that, there is much that heterosexual couples can learn from loving homosexual couples, when it comes to sharing love, not so much in the physical sense, because they have different needs, but in the emotional sense.

As for your next question, Lorelle, as to why the archangels could not just show themselves as more feminine to facilitate a move towards balance by first honouring the female more—it would be possible, but not as effective. Introducing feminine archangels shows the importance that your creator places on helping to create a better balance on your planet.

Living in a Changing World

Today I wanted to talk about life on your planet. You know the world is changing, and you know the reason the world is changing is that you are becoming more loving. As you all become more loving, you are sending more love out into the world, which helps more people become more loving—creating that snowball of love we talked about in your previous book.

Now that the world is becoming more loving, those structures which supported a less loving society are beginning to crumble. You cannot see this from your perspective. Everything seems to you to be just a weird form of normal but trust me when I tell you that things are changing throughout your world. It is up to you all whether those changes are for the better or not, but you can know that your world is changing for the better at the moment, even though it may not seem like it.

You worry that some of your freedoms are being eroded, but your freedom is not an external thing. Your freedom is what you are. You are freedom, because your soul chooses your path and your soul holds your freedom in its hands. Your soul decides what freedoms it allows your physical body and mind to lose or fight for.

You are now at a time in human history where you may have to choose between physical freedom and love. You know that your soul will always choose love. I know that you personally have been having doubts about having a booster vaccination, because you wonder where it will end, how it will end, how will you regain control over your life and your body. Trust me when I say that even though it is possible to lose control of your physical body, it is never possible for you to lose control of your life.

Your soul knew that there would be sacrifices that you may need to make in this physical life, to help bring about the world you desire. You incarnated at this time to help bring more love into the world, and you are doing that. Many of you are doing that.

You cannot know all that is happening behind the scenes, but it is all leading you forward towards your goals. The choices you make along the way towards your goals determine how much benefit you can add. Remember that you need to think love before making any decision and you will always make the right one.

Think love towards your physical body as well, but your body can withstand many hardships, because you can move mountains with sufficient faith. With sufficient faith, you can take a body which has been injected with harsh chemicals and create a perfectly healthy body. You are a child of God and you can create your own reality, including a reality where your body is perfectly healthy.

You know that some of you were born with afflictions or have developed afflictions which may be healed now with sufficient faith. However, your soul may wish to experience life with those afflictions, so may wish to carry on with those. Your soul may also wish to leave behind an afflicted body and return with a brand new body, ready for its next adventure.

Have faith that all will be well, and that everything is happening in divine order. Even if there are events which occur which may not have been orchestrated with the good of All That Is in mind, know that no matter what the situation, the universe must achieve an outcome that benefits All that Is, even if you can't see how that might be possible, also realising that it may not occur at this point in time.

Love is the answer to all questions and if you can make love the determining factor for all that you think, say and do, then the benefit for All That Is is likely to be more immediate.

Now, what sort of world do you wish to create? You, Lorelle, have mentioned to me that you would like world peace, but are you doing everything you can to achieve the world you desire? You mentioned that you wish to improve the oceans and the climate change situation, but are you yourself doing all that you can to achieve that outcome? You know that there is more you can do, even though you have other considerations at the moment. Everyone has other considerations, other priorities, and this is the reason that your goals are taking longer than you hoped, because you all think that someone else needs to do something.

Everyone needs to do the best they can to achieve the goals that you hope for, and thinking love before every thought, word, and deed is the best place to start.

Now, I don't want you to get discouraged. Know that everything is headed in the right direction, and love will soon rule the world. It may just take a little longer than you hoped.

Love is the answer. You are love. You are the answer. That is a big responsibility isn't it, knowing that you are the one responsible? But don't forget that you have much help.

As we talked about previously, you have the help of the archangels and the archaiai, who are overseeing many angels to help achieve your aims. Ask for their help on matters small and large. You sometimes forget. You also have the help of the nature spirits, who are just as determined, or more so, to see the world returned to a more pristine place.

I know you hoped that, with the reduction in greenhouse gases which COVID lockdowns have created due to fewer cruises and flights, the world would be moving more quickly to a pristine state, but there are still many industries having adverse effects on the world—coal fired power stations which pump out air pollution, the fishing industry which contaminates the oceans with fishing gear and clear the oceans of fish which would otherwise feed birds and other animals. Humans are still having short-term and long-term impacts all over the globe—all having detrimental effects on your goals of a more pristine planet.

Have no fear. Things are changing gradually, but you, and those like you who wish to see a better world, can do more to help. You are helping by sending your peace, love, healing and joy out into the world. You are also helping by your food choices. You know that a vegan diet is not only better for your body and the animals, but it is better for the planet in so many ways. Many people are waking up to this fact now, as you have done. There are still a lot more things that you can do to help.

You thought of that today when you walked past some rubbish on the beach. I know you did pick up some, but not all that you saw. It comes down to your priorities, Lorelle. You were worried about dirtying your pockets or your hands, but if you want a cleaner planet, you might have to choose in favour of your planet when you have a choice like that.

Now, Lorelle, I don't want you to think that it is all up to you personally. You can join together with others to pick up rubbish from the beach, just as you can join together with others to send peace, love, healing and joy out into the world.

We are aiming for a world where everyone knows that we are one, that what you do to another being, you do to yourself. Working together to achieve your aims will allow you to celebrate your common goals, while you also acknowledge and celebrate your differences.

It would be wise if all humans realise that having a common goal of a pristine planet would be beneficial to all, and joining forces to work towards that goal would not only move you closer towards your goal of a pristine planet, but would also move you closer towards your goal of everyone knowing that we are one.

Now is the time to get together with those who are like minded to work towards your common goals, even if you only get together on the internet.

You are living in challenging times, but when you think about it, what time in history has not been a challenging time? You have seen a meme about your grandparents living through two world wars, an influenza pandemic, a global recession or depression, as well as other wars and global events. So you know you really don't have it so bad.

The challenges you face are more confusing for you because you haven't lived through it before, but your soul has. Your soul lived through the influenza pandemic. Your soul lived through times of conflict with governments. It lived through many challenging times. It knows what to do. You just need to trust your inner guidance, trust your feelings, which are the voice of your soul.

Lorelle, you have had lessons in following your feelings. You know that to really follow your feelings, you have to put your ego voice to one side.

Your ego will try to tell you that black is white and right is wrong, if it will a) keep you within your comfort zone and b) keep you in fear.

Your ego likes to be in control and it knows that if you start listening to your soul, it won't be needed anymore. In fact, you always need an ego when living in a physical existence, but it doesn't know that. It thinks your soul is trying to kill it, which is why it stays in fear and doesn't like to lose control.

The best way to know if you are really following your feelings is to think love before all that you think, say and do, and to follow the feelings you get after thinking love.

❈❈❈

Helping Animals Help the Planet

Lorelle, you know that there is much to be done to move towards the world you desire, and you know you aren't doing it alone. You have many helpers and you can join with like-minded people to achieve your desires.

You also know that the animals on your planet would love

for you to achieve your aims of bringing veganism more prominently to the world. The animals' roles on the planet are varied. As you know, some have been domesticated and some of those domesticated animals (and some wild animals) have been exploited by humanity in order to turn a profit.

In days of old, the horse collaborated with humans more willingly, as it was playing a necessary part in the evolution of humankind. Horses were valued because of their vital role. Although some were mistreated, they were largely cared for, because of the benefit they provided in everyday life. The same can be said for many domesticated animals, which were once honoured and respected, even if at the ends of their lives they met their death at the hands of humans. Their souls were happy to help, even if the physical being was less so.

Many animals today are not honoured as individuals or as species. Domesticated animals are living life in misery—pigs in sow stalls unable to turn around, chickens cramped together in barns, dairy cows forced to give up their babies time and time again. The examples are endless. Whereas these animals were at one time honoured and respected, they are now seen as stock, nothing more than commodities to be owned and traded, and only kept alive if the expense warrants it.

Wild animals are also being mistreated in a number of ways.

One role that the animals play on your planet has been to provide a balance for the negative energy projected by humans. When you go out in nature, you absorb the positive energy emitted by not only animals, but the trees and other plants as well.

Humans are not only destroying forests and causing the

extinction of many animals, they also change the roles of domestic animals. Whereas previously domestic animals could be relied on to emit positive energy to balance humans' negativity, factory farmed domestic animals particularly, but others too who are not honoured and respected, are no longer emitting this vital positive energy. Rather, they are contributing to the negativity on your planet. How can animals be expected to emit positive energy when they are kept in conditions which cause them abject misery?

Veganism can help return the balance to the planet. It is not only helping with your health, with the animals' health, and with the planet's health, it is helping move the planet towards the New Spirituality, where every person, animal, and Mother Earth herself are treated with respect.

Life on your planet cannot carry on the way it has been, because, as we discussed in your previous book, it will eventually lead to no life on your planet. Your planet is not at risk. It is a powerful being, capable of destroying every human on the Earth. Mother Earth loves you all and would rather not cause any harm to any of its children, however, at some point it will have to make a choice between allowing further destruction or putting a stop to it all. It has a responsibility to all who dwell on her.

Now is the time to take up veganism if you possibly can, or at least vegetarianism. As well as the land animals which will be saved, it will also save the seas from depletion, allowing those animals, who have lost their source of food to humans, to recover, further helping with the essential balance. As we mentioned, fishing gear is a major source of ocean pollution, so this too would be reduced.

Becoming vegan doesn't have to happen overnight. While people continue to consume animals and animal products, there is a need for those who provide this food. It would be a great benefit to the planet, however, if factory farming could be eradicated. While people continue to make money from exploitive farming methods, there is unlikely to be any change. Those people who continue to consume animal products can help the planet in the short term by only consuming free range animals, and preferably organic products which allow for healthier animals.

As you work towards veganism, it would be good if you could honour those animals you do consume, and those who give their lives for the animal products you consume, such as baby cows which die to provide you with cows' milk. I know that this is not something that is practised by many people. Although some might give thanks to God, not many consider the plight of the animals they eat, as they bite into their steaks or drink their milk.

Now that you know the vital roles animals play on your planet, please consider the consequences of every bite of food you take and whether it is necessary to consume animal products at all.

It is not only the food industry where animals are exploited. Wherever animals are used to earn money, there is the risk of exploitation. Please consider how animals are used in your society, and aim to provide them with the best life possible, such that they can once again become contributors to positive energy rather than negative energy.

You are much loved by all beings of love. Your planet is one of those beings. Your mother, the Earth, would love it if all of her offspring could live in harmony together. What will it take for you to consider the consequences of your actions?

Remember that we are here to help you. If you need help to consider the consequences of your actions, ask for help. If you need help to know the consequences, ask and you shall receive.

Love can see you through any difficulties. You know that love is what you are and what you are aiming to see more of on your planet. You can help to bring more love on your planet by thinking love in all that you do. But as we talked about in your previous book, it is not possible to be thinking love if you are thinking violence.

Once you become aware of the violence humans cause to animals, you may not want to think about it. You are an empathic being, and you will feel some of the pain inflicted on animals when you think about it. However, if you never think about it, you cannot be instrumental in changing it. If you are still contributing to violence against animals, it is vital that you consider it, as this is the only way that you can start to change it. It may be painful for you, but it is a necessary step towards change.

Once you are no longer contributing to violence, you no longer need to think about it, unless you can see a role you could play in reducing violence.

❋❋❋

What Would Love Do Now?

Lorelle, tonight I wanted to talk to you about love and how love fits into your lives on Earth. You know from your previous book that love is the same thing as life, which is the same thing as vibration, which is the same thing as sex, as joy, as healing.

The reason love is all those things is because love is all of my creation, but the expression of love can be seen and felt during sex, healing, etc. Now, Lorelle, when you experience love, you wish to share it, as you learned previously. But you know, too, that love makes you feel better, and when you feel enough love, it makes you forget all of your problems, and can make them disappear entirely.

Love will see you through any challenge, will guide you down any path, and will help you be the best that you can be. As we talked about previously, the best that you can be is when you think love, be love, and act with love in all that you do, when you ask "What would love do now?" and when you think love before everything you think, say, and do.

What love would do now may be a different thing for each of you. You can't dictate to others what love would do, because each of you has a different perspective on love; each of you has a different history; and each of you is in a different situation, with different circumstances, different challenges, and different considerations.

It is important to remember that everyone has free will, and you know that my will is that each of you has free will. So, it is not possible to ask what would God do now? and have that as a blanket answer for everyone.

This is indeed what all of your religions have tried to do. They have taken information given as guidance only, and made it a law, with failure to follow that law leading to excommunication or worse.

God is another name for Love, is another name for Life. God allows every being to have free will. Because every being has a different perspective etc, it is not possible to dictate what love would do in each person's case. God gave each of you an internal guidance system, providing you with the feelings we spoke about previously which are the voice of your soul, that part of you closest to God.

If each of you learns to follow your internal guidance system, you are following the voice of God, always bearing in mind that the will of God is that each of you has free will, and free will is paramount.

God doesn't force you to follow your internal guidance system. God merely advises that if you follow your internal guidance system, you are more likely to have an easier life. You may still face challenges, because your soul may desire to learn how to overcome challenges, and learn lessons of love in the process, but those challenges will be easier to overcome when you follow the voice of your soul.

You know, too, that you have many spiritual helpers, and those helpers may also communicate with you through your internal guidance system. In fact, they communicate with you via your soul, so everything that comes through your guidance system comes from your soul.

Now that you know your internal guidance system is the closest thing you can get to the voice of God, you may be wondering why you need external guidance such as this book. You can get by through life using only your internal guidance system, but if you follow your guidance system, you will find that it leads you to information like this, to books like this. It will lead you to all you need to know and learn in this life.

Now that you are aware of your internal guidance system, you may be wondering how you can learn to understand its messages better, and to have conversations such as these for yourself. Previous books of Lorelle's illustrate the path she took to get to where she is today. Even though the books talk about Angela's path, Lorelle's path follows Angela's path, but with a few more pitfalls included, which Lorelle preferred not to include in her books…yet, anyway.

As you know, everyone has free will and with that free will, it is up to you to decide what you do with any information that you receive during your life. Sometimes that information affects others in your life, and you may not wish to share conversations you have with God or other spiritual beings, if it may harm others. This was the decision Lorelle faced, as well as whether it would adversely affect her.

Your inner guidance will help you decide what is in the best interest of all concerned, particularly if you think love before making any decision.

As we discussed, your ego wants to have a say in all that you do, but it may not have the best interests of others in mind, or even your own best interests, for that matter. It is therefore beneficial to endeavour to quieten your ego voice before making important decisions. Your ego can be quietened during meditation and first thing in the morning, before the ego fully awakens. Try making any important decisions during these times. As you know, many people like to make a decision after 'sleeping on it'. This is because you may receive further input from your soul or spiritual helpers while you sleep. You may then awaken with the decision being much more obvious.

Now that you know how to make decisions based on love, there is nothing stopping you. It is possible to align your will with the will of God. In fact, when you do that, you are really asking that your will always acts towards the good of All That Is. However, regardless of what you decide, free will is always paramount. You may find it easier to make decisions in favour of All That Is when you are doing mundane tasks, but life and death decisions, you may find more difficult.

For instance, if you know that your physical death may save the lives of many others, would you choose that?

It is not so easy to know, from your physical perspective, what is in the best interests of All That Is. For instance, if you died today to save those you know you could save today, you may be stopping yourself from achieving something later in your life which may save the planet, or save people from suffering for generations to come.

Your inner guidance system can help you decide, when you think love before your decision. But if you can't know the best course of action for yourself, how can you possibly know the best course of action for another? This is one reason we ask you not to judge others—because you cannot possibly know, from your limited perspective, what is in the best interests of that person and the best way for them to contribute to All That Is.

You can use your internal guidance system to advise people if they ask for help, but if they don't ask for help, they may already have all the help they need within.

Do you see how it works?

The universe was designed as a beneficial universe. It will always provide you with your desires in alignment with the best possible scenario for All That Is. However, free will is paramount, so the universe cannot override your or anyone else's free will.

If you align your will with the best possible scenario for All That Is, it makes the universe's job much easier, and usually will provide a better solution for you, as part of that All That Is.

Life was meant to be fun. Life was meant to be enjoyed. Life was meant to be easy.

You can certainly make it easier for yourself by following your internal guidance system and thinking love before all that you do. But you can also make it easier by aligning your will with God's will, which is that everyone has the best possible life they possibly can, including you.

But with your free will, you get to decide the kind of life you have. Your soul is in charge, and it is not always possible for you to know the outcome your soul desires, but it will certainly be easier if you listen during meditation and by following your feelings.

Go now, and consider what you think might be in the best interests of All That Is.

❄❄❄

Helping The Planet

We have talked about veganism and how you can help the planet with this dietary choice. But there are many other ways you can help the planet.

When you think love before all that you do, your actions are more likely to help the planet than if you do everything without thinking love. Now imagine all you can accomplish when you put your miraculous power of love to work in more intense ways.

Firstly, you can ask for ideas on ways to help the planet. As you meditate you can receive information from your guides and higher self about ways that you can help, and your spiritual helpers can then be instrumental in putting signs in your path leading you towards that goal.

You can put love to work in social settings by spreading the word about the miraculous power of love.

You can allow love to guide you throughout all of your life in all that you do.

You know that Mother Earth loves all of her children, including you. Keeping in touch with Mother Earth, literally if you can, will remind you to put her higher up the priority list, but it will also allow you to feel her love.

You can also send your peace, love, healing and joy out into the world—to all the people and creatures of the Earth and to Mother Earth herself.

As you interact with Mother Earth, you get to feel the love she has for you and all of her beings. As you send out love to everyone on Earth and to Mother Earth, you receive it back tenfold.

As you can see, there are many ways you can help the planet, just by using the love within you. When you start to project that love outward into all you do, you can work even more miracles.

Now that you know the power of love to affect the future of the planet and all who dwell upon her, what else can you turn your hand to, or turn your love to?

You know that we discussed in your previous book what life might be like in the New Spirituality, and we mentioned that highly evolved beings (HEBs) will come to help you on your planet when the time is right. This is beginning to happen now. Some of you are already in discussion with these beings. Some of you will receive telepathic messages such as these. Some will receive visits. Others will be asked to take journeys with them to learn about their ways of doing things.

The main thing they will teach you will be how to be more loving. Even though we are teaching you with this book and other methods about love and how to use it in the world, these HEBs will provide practical advice on using your love to create the outcomes you desire, both in your personal lives and on a global scale.

There are also many spiritual helpers helping you and your planet at this time. We mentioned the archangels and archaiai, but other realms are all joining forces to help you in many ways now. You just have to ask and you will receive the help you desire.

But as I said previously, even though you have much help, you still need to take personal responsibility for all that you think, say, and do, and to ensure that those aspects of you are all working to achieve your aims.

But what are your aims?

Are your aims for a peaceful world where everyone—animals, people and Mother Earth—are all treated with respect? You can work with others whose aims are the same to help achieve this goal.

Remember to ask and you shall receive. But you can ask for more than you have thought. Rather than asking for a peaceful world where everyone is treated with respect, you can ask for that, but also ask that everyone is working towards those aims with everything, they think, say, and do.

What if your desires are slightly different to Lorelle's? Perhaps you want a peaceful world, but don't care about the planet or the animals. You might be surprised to learn that you can't really have one without the other. And you probably have worked out the reason by now—we are all one.

You cannot have peace amongst humans and keep animals living in fear and misery. You can't have a peaceful world while you continue to destroy all the rainforests and the rest of the habitats for the Earth's species.

Lorelle learned how everything is linked in her biology class. The plants create your oxygen; without them you cannot survive and every species on the planet has a role linking it to some other part of the web of life on the planet. If you destroy enough of that web, there will be no more life on the planet.

Your mother, the Earth, knows how connected life is. She also knows that many of your industries are not sustainable—the ones which pollute the Earth's water tables, the ones which pollute the Earth's oceans, the ones which kill the world's bees; the list is long.

Your species is awakening to the effects you are having on your biosphere, but you still haven't grasped the gravity of the situation. You think you can carry on as you always have or even increase your harmful behaviours and someone else will sort things out.

Someone else will install solar panels; someone else will use the electric car; someone else will pick up the rubbish…always someone else. We are one. What you do to another, you do to yourself. What you fail to do for another, you fail to do for yourself.

This is your Earth, your home. You toilet train your pets not to mess in the home, but you haven't learned that your home is more than your house. Your home is the planet you live on, and you are pooping all over it. Sometimes literally. Sometimes raw effluent enters the oceans that provide your seafood. Your livestock pollute creeks and rivers which run into the ocean, causing toxic algae to thrive and kill other species. You know the consequences of your actions in most cases and yet you let these consequences continue.

"But it's not me!" I hear you say. "It's my government, my supplier, someone else." But who votes for the government? Who buys from that supplier? Who is that someone else?

It is time now to consider the consequences of your actions in all that you do, but also all that you don't do.

Could you have signed that petition? Could you have written that letter? Could you have stopped buying from that supplier and told them why? Could you have talked to that someone else and explained the consequences of their actions and why they might want to reconsider?

"But you said we can't know what their soul wants of them."

No, but if they are working in ways which are harmful to your planet and All That Is, chances are they are not listening to their souls. Your voice may be the catalyst they need to start them listening, but think love before you say or do anything.

❊❊❊

Life in the New Spirituality

Lorelle, today we wanted to talk to you about all that will be happening to you in the near future. I know we discussed this previously in your earlier book, but not everyone has read that, and they may want a reminder.

You know that we talked about the world that is to come in Tomorrow's God[16] *by Neale Donald Walsch. You know that we called this new world the New Spirituality, because that is the state of affairs that will be on your planet then, which will be soon, if you all can do it by thinking love more.*

We told you about all the changes that would happen in the New Spirituality. We talked about the way education would change to focus on the new Three Rs: Reconciliation, Re-creation, and Reunification. You know we talked about sex and birth control, and the change in focus for people on your planet, as they learn to talk more about sex, and view it as the natural and loving act that it is, making it less of a focus for everyone. We talked about the need to reduce the population of humans by birth control, until you have learned to control your reproduction with your minds.

You know you are all working to bring about the New Spirituality. We mentioned before that it is one of your aims, Lorelle, and hopefully that of your readers.

The New Spirituality will see you all much happier because you will better understand your role in life when you have a closer association with your higher self and your spiritual helpers. This association will see you feeling joy more often. When you follow your feelings which are the voice of your soul, they lead you away from discomfort towards joy. Once you have all learned what it feels like to follow the voice of your soul, you will be able to do it more and more often, meaning that you will be living in joy more often.

Won't that be wonderful?

You remember from your previous book, Lorelle, that we hoped your readers and others in the world would also begin to have a closer association with God. Some of you already have a close relationship with me, because your soul would lead you towards that if you are listening to it, unless it doesn't. Sometimes your soul has other scenarios it needs to encounter first, and things it wants to achieve. But sooner or later, your soul will lead you to me.

Your ego will fight this of course. Your ego will think that it will be killed as you come closer to God. It fact, your ego is silenced more and more, the closer you come to God, but as you recede away again, your ego is still intact, ready to help you get along in the world and help you achieve your goals.

That is the purpose of the ego. You are designed to be ruled by your soul, and your ego is meant to help your soul achieve its aims during your lifetime. Sometimes, however, usually in fact, your ego is given control over your being, which can lead you away from joy and towards fear. Your ego will usually try to lead you away from God as well.

As we mentioned in your previous books, Lorelle, it would be wonderful if now people on your planet could have a closer relationship with God. God can teach you how to experience the love that dwells within you and also allow you to feel a small part of the love which I am. I am that I am. I am love. I am you. I am everything. Everything is made of love. I can allow you to feel some of my vast stores of love, if you ask me. You might need some preparatory steps, but soon you could be immersing yourself in the honey pot of ecstasy, just as Lorelle did.

As she pointed out in her previous book, when she moved closer to that honey pot of ecstasy, she forgot all about her problems, and in fact her problems completely disappeared. As we discussed then, after much training it is possible to get to a stage of being able to come and experience a vast amount of love for a while, and then return to whatever you were being or doing but feeling much more joyful afterwards.

How many of you would like to experience such joy, such ecstasy, such love?

It is yours for the asking. Ask and you shall receive.

These are some of the joys that await you in the New Spirituality.

You know that your spiritual helpers—all the angels, spirit guides, Ascended Masters, and light beings—will be available to help just as they are now. But whereas now, very few of you have awareness of these beings, and then only partial awareness, in time to come you will all have a closer relationship with these spiritual helpers.

Your ancestors will be more accessible to you as well. As you know, your ancestors go on to other love lessons, passing on to the realm of deceased loved ones from the life you knew them in. They may have gone on to other physical lives or returned to the spirit realm where they learn more about love, as they prepare for returning to Earth or another planet at another time. They may become spirit guides or take on other roles which have absolutely no relationship to their previous role on your planet.

Depending on their current role, they will be readily accessible in the New Spirituality. If you call to them, they will leave what they are being or doing and come to you. Your soul is in lots of places and times at once. Your soul is everywhere.

Your life in the New Spirituality will be filled with love. Your life now is filled with love, but sometimes you don't experience it. In the New Spirituality you will experience so much love—love from within, love from your ancestors, love from your spiritual helpers, love from God, and love from other humans, animals, plants and Mother Earth.

What a joyous place it will be, don't you think?

Now that you understand all that you have to look forward to, you can appreciate the need to work towards the New Spirituality as fast as possible. And love is the key.

As we mentioned in your previous book, work will look different in the New Spirituality as well. It is more likely to be called employment, because it will no longer be seen as work, but for most it will be fun.

Even those employed in menial tasks such as toilet cleaning, will feel greater joy in their work, as they understand that to bring out the joy in themselves, they just need to bring out the joy in another. People will appreciate a job well done and find joy in the service provided to them and the service provided by them.

People will follow the voice of their souls, so they will be normally following their passion. If their passion is to buy a small business for instance, their soul may lead them to clean toilets in the meantime, as a means to an end. As people will be more in touch with their souls, their higher selves, they will understand that toilet cleaning is merely a steppingstone on the path to their passion, and will find joy in their employment in the service of others and in the service of their longer term goals.

This is just an example. Everyone will find the employment they desire, even if it is not the employment they wish to spend the rest of their life in.

Life will be filled with joy, because you are joy; you will be just in a position to experience it more often.

Now that you know what you can look forward to, won't you be keen to bring about the New Spirituality as soon as possible?

You can start now by meditating often. During meditation you can hear the voice of your higher self and your spiritual helpers. You can learn to follow your feelings, as Lorelle has done. It is merely a lesson in listening to your body. Unlike Lorelle, you may already have a close relationship with your body. When we started on Lorelle's lessons, she was not accustomed to listening to what her body was telling her, and when she did listen, she didn't know what it was trying to tell her.

Yoga classes was one way she learned to listen to her body, and her spiritual helpers and I helped her to understand what it was trying to tell her. It just took a little practice. You, too, can learn these things easily. Ask and you shall receive.

Now that you have learned to follow the voice of your soul by meditating regularly and following your feelings, you are sure to be feeling joy more often. Lots of people will want to try this now, don't you think?

The New Spirituality is a time in the near future when

everyone will get along. Yes, there may be disagreements, but rather than settling disagreements with war and fighting, those disagreements will be settled with discussion and compromise.

Everyone will know that we are one, and that what you do to another, you do to yourself, so there is no point settling differences with war or conflict. Everyone will know that what goes around comes around. Everyone will want to settle things with love not war. Everyone will ask: 'What would love do now?' Everyone will think love, be love, and act with love. Everyone will think love before everything they think, say and do.

You are all a joy to me, and it would be my pleasure for you to experience the joy that you are. The New Spirituality will help you do that.

What would you like to do now?

Would you like to move towards the New Spirituality as quickly as possible? Sign up here then. Sign up to be a beacon of love and light to all the world. Sign up to help the people of the world remember who they are—beacons of light and love themselves. As you share your light and love with others, you remind them to look within for their own light and love. You can help them find the help they need by letting them know how you came to remember your light and love. Sharing your light and love and sharing your source of the means of remembering who you are will help bring the New Spirituality to the Earth as quickly as possible.

Go now and be my beacon of light and love to all the world. Be at peace.

❄❄❄

Understanding Consciousness

God, you said: *"Sometimes, however, usually in fact, your ego is given control over your being, which can lead you away from joy and towards fear."*

Who gives the ego control? Who is the you, you spoke of? You said we are three-part beings and the soul is in charge. So does the soul give the ego control?

No, your consciousness. Your consciousness is a mixture of influence from your mind and soul, and to a much lesser extent your body. Your consciousness is determined by how awake you are. If you are fully awake, you are generally giving control to your soul. If you are fully asleep, you are generally giving control to your ego. If you are partially awake, you alternate between the two.

Unfortunately, many people on your planet are not yet awake, and those that are awake are not fully awake.

You said that you are giving control to your ego if you are asleep, but you said that the soul determines when it will need to awaken after first carrying out the things it needs to achieve in a sleeping state. So, doesn't that mean that the soul gives the ego control?

Yes, in that situation. But remember we said that some people are able to awaken now, but they are just sleeping more soundly.

So, who keeps the person sleeping soundly?

You do, Lorelle. It is hard for you to understand.

There is a piece of the puzzle missing, God.

You cannot understand because you are not fully awake. If you were fully awake, it would make complete sense to you.

I am trying to understand. The soul keeps the person asleep until it has completed its pre-awakening achievements. Then it says, "Right, you can wake up now." But the person doesn't wake up. So which part of the being—body, mind, or soul is asleep?

None of those parts, Lorelle.

My consciousness decides?

No, Lorelle, my consciousness decides.

God decides when I wake up?

No, your ability to wake up is determined by your soul, but I give your soul guidelines about when you can wake up. Those guidelines are based on what you want to achieve in your life.
Consciousness is the essence of us all. It is what your ego fears to lose, and what your God and your soul want to experience. Consciousness is what makes us one. If we weren't conscious, we

would have to be separate. Yet, as you experienced, as you come closer to God, your consciousness is only aware of love. To be conscious, you have to separate yourself from God. Otherwise, you are only conscious of love.

"If we weren't conscious, we would have to be separate." The ego is wanting to be separate and acts unconsciously. God wants to experience consciousness by becoming separate beings. Does this make sense?

No, it makes no sense to your ego mind, which is the one asking the question. It cannot understand consciousness because it is not conscious. Your God mind is not conscious when it is in God. It is only conscious when it is in you, in its separate beings. When it is God, it is only love and conscious only of love.

I'm sorry I asked this question.

I know. You can sleep on it if you wish.

Yes, please. But before I do, the question came from the message that we need to give our ego less control and our soul more. How do we go about doing that?

You make a conscious choice to give control to your soul. Your conscious choice is made by your consciousness. It is your consciousness which sets the intention you wish to achieve. Your consciousness is where you and I meet. Your three-part being and my All That Is meet in your consciousness.

Wouldn't that be a fourth part then?

No. As I said before, consciousness is what makes us one. So when you are conscious, you are only one, not three.

But as I came closer to the One, I lost consciousness of anything but love. Wow, is this starting to make sense just a little? I'll sleep now, and come back to it, ok?

Ok.

❄❄❄

God, you know you confused me last night.

I know, Lorelle, but we'll sort it out tonight.

Good.

Firstly, God, You said the soul wants to experience consciousness. I understand God wanting to experience consciousness, so God created conscious beings. But I thought a soul is conscious.

No, Lorelle. Remember I told you that the soul is that part of you most like God—closest to God. Well, the soul is conscious only through its physical incarnations.

Well, do I have a different understanding of consciousness then, because I thought consciousness was being aware? So is a soul not aware? Jesus said he experiences nothing but joy in his current state. And you said that souls have 'thoughts' of a sort. I assumed that our spirit guides are souls in spirit not in physical and are aware.

Yes, Lorelle, your soul is aware of itself in the spiritual realm and aware of God. But its awareness doesn't have any bearing on anything until it is conscious, and it is not conscious until it is physical.

So consciousness is not awareness?

No.

So, what is consciousness?

Consciousness, as I said, is where you and I meet. It is where your three-part being and God meet.

And what is the definition of being conscious then?

To be conscious is to be aware of life within your being. Although a soul in spirit is aware of life around it, it is unaware of life within itself until it manifests in the physical.

You were saying about lessons that we have in spirit. Do we not need to be conscious to have such lessons?

No, you only need to be conscious to apply those life lessons.

To apply life lessons, you need to be conscious of the consequences of your actions.

You said that in spirit souls soon learn to only have positive 'thoughts' because they manifest the consequences immediately.

Yes, there are still consequences of 'thought' in spirit, but to be conscious of those consequences, you need to apply those thoughts in the physical realm.

So, are you saying that only souls which have physical beings can understand the consequences of their 'thoughts'?

No, souls can only act on their thoughts in the physical realm. Even though they have immediate consequences of their 'thoughts' in the spirit realm, they are not conscious of the consequences until they act on them in the physical realm.

You said that to apply our life lessons, we need to be conscious of the consequences of our actions. But you said that most of us, when the ego is in control, are not conscious of the consequences of our actions.

That is right, Lorelle.

I am getting close to giving up on trying to understand this, God. I thought that everything happens for a reason. But it is difficult for me to turn off my mind to listen to you and turn it back on to think and make sense of what you have told me.

I know, Lorelle. We can come back to it again later. You had some other questions.

Can you explain: "If we weren't conscious, we would have to be separate"?

Yes, Lorelle. You are a three-part being and I am All That Is. Your three-part being is only conscious when it is connected to God. God is only conscious of anything other than love when it is connected to you and the rest of my creation.

Ok, God. I'll take your word for that. Can you tell me what is the difference between awareness and consciousness?

Yes, Lorelle. Your awareness of your surroundings and your being becomes conscious when you are in touch with God via your soul. Your soul is aware of your three-part being only because it is connected to God, which makes its awareness become conscious.

"Souls have immediate consequences of their 'thoughts' in the spirit realm." Are they aware of these consequences?

Not in the same way the physical being is aware. The consequences do not have negative or positive effects on the soul as they do in the physical realm, but the soul still becomes aware that it is a consequence that needs to be embraced or avoided. Thus, the soul still learns from these consequences, even though they do not feel they are positively or negatively affected by them.

Ok, God, that's all my questions about consciousness, but I wonder if the readers might not have further questions.

Yes, Lorelle. You can ask your readers to ask me directly any questions they still have about consciousness or anything in this book, and request they relate the answers to you. You may still not be able to completely understand, but there may be further glimmers of understanding.

❄︎ ❄︎ ❄︎

Creating With Love and Faith

Today I wanted to talk about love again, because, as you know, love is all there is.
Love is what we all are made of. Love is the power I use to create worlds. You are made of love also. So could you create worlds with the power of your love?
Yes and no.
Have I not told you that with sufficient faith you can move mountains? Most of you, unfortunately, don't have sufficient faith. But in some ways that is good. Imagine the chaos you could create if you had faith but didn't apply that faith with love. You are powerful beings, and you can create miracles. But you can also create mayhem.

It is important to use both love and faith when creating. You know the stories of Jesus and the miracles he performed. He was able to use love and faith to create miracles. And you can too.

Just as you may need some preparatory steps in other areas of your development, you may need preparatory steps in your creation lessons.

This is one reason why it would be good to bring about the New Spirituality method of teaching—both children and adults. The method of education we spoke of in Tomorrow's God[17] *uses these tools of love and faith to create a platform for education. Every other lesson is based on these lessons.*

Once you and your children have these fundamental building blocks, it is far safer to let them and you loose into the world to create the world of your desire.

Can you imagine the chaos which could ensue if people were creating without these basic fundamentals? That is close to the world you have today. Civilisations, if you can call them that, based not on love, but on greed, for the most part.

Even though everything is made of love and everything in its essence is an expression of love, greed does not express a love of All That Is, only an expression of love for the small self.

Once you understand the law of attraction, you can start to attract the world of your dreams. But without a love for All That Is, you can create a bit of a mess. You can create a world where you get what you want today, but cause so many ripples out into the world that the consequences of those dreams coming to you can cause a lot more pain and suffering in the long term. This is the way many of you are creating now or have created in the past.

You have forgotten the golden rule which says: do unto others as you would have them do unto you. This includes all the beings on the planet, including Mother Earth. What goes around comes around. If you are not careful, your dreams today can cause you a lot of suffering in the future.

You don't realise how powerful you are. It is understandable that you wish to see yourself as happy, and you believe that what you desire at this time will bring you happiness. But when it comes, are you happy?

Your new car, your new house, that higher salary in your job—does all this bring you happiness?

It may for a time, but only if you are following your feelings, only desiring those things which will bring you closer to your soul's aims.

You are so powerful, you can create worlds. You can create the world you live in to be however you wish it to be. If your desires are based on your soul's desires, they are likely to be in keeping with your highest good and the highest good for All That Is. If your desires are based on your ego's thoughts and wants, you may end up being disappointed sooner rather than later, and in the long run, depending on the consequences, you may end up suffering.

Now that you realise the power you have, you just need to remember to think love before offering your desires, and it is likely to be a loving desire. Meditate often and you will be in harmony with your soul's desires, which are likely to be in harmony with All That Is.

So perhaps your first thought, when deciding what sort of world you would like to create, should be love. Once you have thought love, your next thought perhaps could be to ask: 'What would serve All That Is at this time?' This is just another way of asking: 'What would love do now?' Because love would serve All That Is.

Don't forget that you are part of All That Is, so wanting the best for All That Is does not mean you need to sacrifice anything. It just means aligning your little self desires with your Big Self desires.

It is not hard. It just takes practice.

Once you start thinking love before all you think, say, and do, you are well on the way to creating the world that would benefit All That Is.

However, once you start off that way, you may have lapses along the way. Once your ego gets involved, you may start to think that you are so special now that you don't need any more lessons or any more practice, and this is where you fall down. Your ego is helping you become the person your soul desires you to be by providing you with opportunities to practise falling down and getting back up, stronger than before.

Humility will help you on this path. But then your ego will start to tell you that you are humble, so you will start to feel special for being so humble. Here comes another lesson and more practice.

So, even though lessons of love and faith are easy at their essence, they can be hard to get right consistently, as Lorelle can attest. She is still learning, as you all are. But she is getting better, as you all are.

Each setback is overcome. Sometimes it will feel like one step forward and two steps back, but in fact it is more likely to be one step back and two steps forward. You are always improving. You are always getting better at your lessons, even if it seems you have climbed a high mountain and fallen to the bottom, only to start the climb all over again. Your progress is always up.

Remember everyone is different, and everyone's path is different. Some move ahead in leaps and bounds, only to fall at the last hurdle. Some take the slow and steady path and arrive at the top of the mountain ahead. Others want to stop along the path and enjoy the view for a while.

Please don't judge others on their path. Neither judge yourself harshly, as Lorelle has done on occasion.

Jesus told you to love others as yourself. You need to cut yourself the same slack you would for others.

You are all doing the best you can in the situation in which you find yourself. You are all my beloved children, all learning how to be God, which is another name for love.

Violence in Society

What we wanted to talk about now was what you need to do to get to where you want to go. As we mentioned, veganism is one way of helping the world move forward, but one of the reasons for that was to remove violence from your world.

There is so much violence inflicted on animals, not only food animals, but race horses, brumbies, circus animals, foie gras geese, down ducks—there is a long list. You can do your bit by not buying any of these products.

But there is a lot of violence among humans as well. This is harder to eradicate.

There is violence in sport, on television, and on electronic games, and these can be phased out once the will is there, and people stop supporting these activities but what about the violence endemic in societies?

Some less evolved countries still have capital punishment, including the United States of America.

That is correct. The USA is one of the least evolved nations on your planet. As we learned, Highly Evolved Beings (HEBs) would not consider killing someone as a suitable punishment for any crime. In fact, HEBs wouldn't consider punishment at all. They might consider keeping an offender under control so that they couldn't harm anyone else, but they would do so with the aim of rehabilitating the person, knowing that in most cases, violent offenders have been the victims of violence themselves. Rather than punishment, they would deal with these people with love, as they deal with any problem that arises.

There is so much violence in your world that you take it so much for granted. But you cannot bring about world peace while you continue to promote violence, inflict violence, and watch violence.

Your military is another example. Your military personnel are trained to kill. They are trained not to listen to their inner guidance which would tell them to at least stop and ask: Is this necessary? What would love do now?

Yes, there are times when it may be necessary to kill in order to maintain peace, but those times are very few. Your nations' leaders have been all too quick to use force against other nations and against other entities by whom they feel threatened.

One has to ask, however: Why do you feel threatened? What is the goal of an enemy which threatens you? Is there another means of them achieving their goal? What would love do now?

It is unlikely that any industry which makes for its owners millions of dollars could be eradicated without the will of millions of people who elect a government based on love rather than money.

Many of your government bodies' elected officials are supported by industries which support violence, whether violence to humans, animals, or Mother Earth.

So what can you do about it?

You can make yourself aware of the political processes in your country. Make yourself aware of the means to change those political processes. Make yourself aware of the industries supporting your elected officials. Don't vote for violence. Vote for those who offer to change the processes.

Be the Change

There is much that you can do to help bring about world peace. You are all peace. You all just need to be what you are.

Even those who are listening to their inner guidance, at times allow their egos to muffle the voice of their higher selves, particularly when it comes to going against the trend.

Your ego doesn't want to stand out. Your ego wants to be accepted and go along with the status quo. It is safer. It doesn't feel threatened that way.

You can follow Jesus' example. Even though he followed the law and the prophets, he didn't allow traditions of his community to dictate his activities. He fed people on the Sabbath, he turned the money lenders out from the temple, he told people to give unto Caesar that which was Caesar's at a time when others wanted to rebel, he stopped a woman from being stoned by the masses.

To follow Jesus' example, you not only have to remember to think love before all that you do. You have to stand out from the crowd, unless you fortunately happen to be with a crowd of people who are also thinking love often.

Now that you know that there is so much that needs to change, you may start to feel discouraged, but even though there are a lot of things on your planet not in alignment with your goal of world peace, the solution is the same for all of the issues and problems: more love. You just need to be who you are. You are peace, love, healing, and joy incarnate. You are freedom. You are life. You are God.

You are humans endeavouring to be more God-like, but at your essence, you are love. You have been created using the stuff of God, which is love. You just have to be what you are. How hard can that be?

It is easy, particularly with all the help you are receiving. And once you realise what you are, it is in your best interests to remind others of what they are.

Love will overcome any difficulties. Step from your comfort zone, come out of the closet, and shine your light and love out into the world for all to see. It is easier to hide behind others, to blend in, to not stand out. But is it?

Your feelings tell you to be a beacon. It is only your ego telling you to hide your light. Your soul wants you to shout it from the rooftops: "I am love and so are you. We are love. We are one."

Now don't be afraid to stand on that mountain top and shine your light for all to see. You have many people who have gone before you. Not only Jesus, but many in your current times. Would you like me to name a few names?

The Dalai Lama. Wayne Dyer. Lorelle Taylor.

Oops. Lorelle is having trouble writing that, because, just like you, she doesn't want to be the one to stand out. She has learned that she is no more special than anyone else, so she doesn't want to be singled out. But that is my point. None of these people are more special than you. Each of you has a role to play in bringing about the new world that you wish for. Each of you has been given a way to shine your light into the world. Each of you is a role model to others.

What sort of role model do you want to be?

What sort of legacy do you wish to leave?

Would you like to be the one who bought that extra luxurious car, or the one who found a way to bring more love into the world?

In the words of Mahatma Gandhi, you need to be the change you wish to see in the world. If you desire a more loving world, you need to be more loving. If you desire a more peaceful world, you need to be more peaceful.

Now that you know what is required of you, are you up to the task?

You came into the world at this time knowing the demands that would be placed on you, but knowing, too, the joy it would bring you. Follow your joy to the end of the rainbow, where your desire of a peaceful world awaits you.

Now that you know you are here on a mission, are you willing to take up that mission?

You have free will, and you can accept or reject this mission at any time. But now that you know that it will bring you joy, isn't it worth it?

❄❄❄

Sex

We discussed sex in your previous books, but today I wanted to talk about what people are missing out on in their sex lives. For some reason, your religions decided that sex is a bad thing or even a sin, unless done in the cause of procreation. Attitudes are changing in some areas of your religious bodies, but there is still a stigma from previous teachings.

Sex is a wonderful expression of love. Even the birds and bees do it. Animals understand that it is a natural thing. Yes, they instinctively aim to further their species and protect their genes, even though they don't think this consciously. However, in their quest to further their species and protect their genes, they enjoy their moments of passion. However, sex between humans can be so much more than an animalistic act. It can take you closer to God.

You know that during climax, you sometimes shout "Oh God!" Well God is there always when you call. Remember that you cannot use the Lord's name in vain. This doesn't mean that you can't speak my name; this means that I am with you always, especially when you call my name.

But I digress.

Sex between two humans can be a way for both parties to experience feelings close to ecstasy.

If you have read Lorelle's previous books, you will remember that Angela felt close to ecstasy as she came close to God—the honeypot in our analogy. You will remember that Angela told you that she felt her problems disappear as she came closer to God. The same happens when you are having sex. Your daily concerns disappear, and you are left only with joy and love, and close to ecstasy if you are lucky. This is in an ideal scenario.

Unfortunately, many people fail to experience all these wonderful feelings. They often have so many hang-ups about sex passed down to them from earlier generations, that they fail to let go of their concerns and fail to experience the joy that is available to them.

So what is the answer?

As usual, more love. But usually not in the bedroom.

When you are young, your hormones allow you to have engaging sex, regardless. But as you age and your hormones reduce, sex often becomes something that is expected of you. For a man, it is seen as a means of loving oneself, instead of masturbation. For a woman, it is seen as a way to express love to her man, even if she is not in the mood.

I am talking in generalisations here. Everyone is different. Everyone has different sex drives, but many men do not really understand a woman's sex drives.

Women need love in order to have loving sex. But rarely is it in the bedroom that they desire this love. I am not saying to take your sex to the lounge room or the bathroom. I am saying that women desire love while getting dinner, while bathing the children, or while doing any of the other multitude of things they do throughout their day. They require a loving touch when they are sitting relaxing or when washing the dishes; they could use some help when making the bed. They need more love throughout their day. When they feel loved, they are more able to offer love in return, in the form that men desire.

But the same thing applies to a lesser extent to men. They, too, require love throughout their day.

So sex doesn't originate in the bedroom, or at least the enjoyment of it doesn't. The enjoyment of love starts a long time before.

So what can you do to enjoy sex more?

Find a partner, I hear someone say. And yes, it is nice to have a partner for sex, but as we discussed in previous books, loving yourself physically can still bring you close to ecstasy, if you truly love yourself emotionally as well. So, even when loving yourself, sex doesn't start in the bedroom.

It starts during those times when, instead of telling yourself you're useless, you congratulate yourself on how well you have done to try. Instead of frowning at yourself when you look in the mirror, you could tell yourself, "I love you. You are beautiful/handsome."

Love for yourself is necessary to have sufficient love to share. If you are unable to love yourself, you start to look for love outside yourself. Instead, you need to look for love within. When you find your love within, you then have enough love to share.

❄❄❄

Learning to Love Yourself

Sex is a joyful expression of love between a man and a woman or sometimes between same sex couples. Sex can be joyful, but even though it is often enjoyed by humans, it usually falls short of its possibilities.

It is possible to have orgasm after orgasm, as we mentioned in your previous book. The best way to achieve this is to love yourself first—both physically and emotionally. When you love yourself first, you have more love to share and when you feel your love within, you can't help but want to share it.

However, you have not been taught how to love yourself, either physically or emotionally. Your parents generally teach you the opposite—how to dislike yourself. You have had lessons in disliking yourself from your religions as well. So how can you overcome these lessons and start teaching yourself how to love yourself?

In your current state of development, it would be considered wrong to show your children how you love yourself physically, and that may be more of a hindrance than a help if you did that anyway, given that you weren't taught the best way yourself.

Teach yourself first how to love yourself emotionally. Once you can do that, your physical expression of love for yourself will come much more easily to you. Showing your children how to love yourself emotionally is also permissible in your current state of development.

The first thing to remember is to think love before anything you do. There are vast resources available about how to love yourself emotionally, and if you ask your spiritual helpers, they will introduce you to those which will benefit you the most. You may need a hypnotherapist, or perhaps a book to get started. Each of you has different needs, because each of you has a different history and therefore different teachings from parents and religions that you first need to overcome.

Once you can love yourself emotionally, you are in a better position to create an atmosphere in your home where your children can love themselves emotionally without any lessons. If they do require lessons, they may require different forms of help than you did. Depending on their age, they can ask their own spiritual helpers, or you can ask on their behalf if they are young.

Once you can love yourself emotionally, you can begin to learn to love yourself physically. Here too, you can ask your spiritual helpers for help with this.

Most of you have never been shown the best way to pleasure yourself, so make this your aim: to know and love yourself first, then to share your love with your partner in a way that pleases them best, while they share their love with you in a way which best pleases you.

Communication is the key. You need to talk about sex. Sex between two people can be a joyful thing leading to ecstasy, but you will be less likely to achieve the best of sex if you can't tell your mate how you want to be loved. If you have no idea how you like to be loved because you have never loved yourself physically, it is more difficult.

Usually men have more practice of self-love, but often they have forgotten to love themselves emotionally first, so their joy is often less than it could be during physical self-love. Once you can love yourself emotionally, you can find more joy when loving yourself physically, and then share that joy with your partner, when you share your love both emotionally and physically.

So where to start?

Start by looking in the mirror. What do you see? Do you see wrinkles, or a loving soul looking out through your eyes?

If you can look yourself in the eyes, you will see love shining out. When you see that love, it is possible then to say to yourself, "I love you."

If you can speak these words without looking away, you are ready to move on to lesson 2. If you need to look away, or can't bring yourself to say I love you, keep practising this.

Lesson 2 comes from your spiritual helpers, who will find you the perfect means of moving towards the self-love you desire and set you on the path towards physical love for yourself and another, which will lead you to ecstasy.

Sex is always a difficult subject to approach in discussions, because you all have varying degrees of complexes about sex. Your society has made sex a taboo subject, which has only recently started to change.

In order to keep the trend heading in the right direction, it is a good idea to talk about sex at every opportunity—with your partner particularly, but with your friends as well.

God encourages sex, because sex actually brings you closer to me. During sex, you usually can leave your ego mind to one side and follow your feelings, which as you remember are the voice of your soul. Your soul wants you to come closer to God. The love you feel during sex is your love expressed, but your love is my love, and you are pleasing God. We are one.

Now that you know that loving your partner is loving God,

you may feel a little awkward. Most people separate God from their sex lives. God is someone to worship on Sundays at best, or someone who is not considered at all. Knowing that you are getting closer to God during sex may seem a bit strange at first but remember that I invented sex. I gave each of you a way to provide yourself and your partner pleasure and love while getting closer to God. God is always with you, no matter what you do. You just experience God more during sex, particularly joyful loving sex.

❆❆❆

Peace

We spoke about sex, but now we need to talk about something closer to your heart—peace. For peace does indeed emanate from your heart. Your peace comes from within, just as your love does. Once you find your peace within, you can share that with the world or your partner, just as you do your love.

So how do you find your peace? Go within. As well as getting in touch with your higher self during meditation, you can also get in touch with your heart, which leads you to the heart of the matter. The heart of the matter you are all working towards is world peace. You are trying to change the world out there, but first you need the change the world within.

Even though you are peace and your heart emits peace, you put up barricades and blockages which stop your heart from emitting peace. You search for peace outside yourself, and you find it—in bodies of water, in nature, in pets. This is because those beings have not blocked the emission of their peace.

The only animals who block their emission of peace are humans, and those who have been forced to by humans. Those are the animals who turn on their handlers in circuses, who kill hunters, or are trapped in cages (blockages and barricades). Otherwise, animals emit peace.

Your world peace cannot be achieved without removing the blockages and barricades you have erected, firstly within yourself, and then wherever you have erected them. Now that you know where to find peace, how do you go about removing your blockages and barricades? As always—more love.

If your heart tells you to rest, your blockage may stop you from hearing. If your heart tells you to love others, your blockage may decide to hate instead. Your heart tells you there is nothing to fear in this world or the next but your blockage keeps you in fear.

You see a pattern here? Your ego is the cause of your blockages and barricades within, and the reason you have created them without. Without them, you would be free, as would those you have barricaded in.

So how do you remove your barricades? Love: by thinking love before everything you think, say, and do; by meditating regularly to stay in touch with your higher self; and by listening to your feelings, which are the voice of your soul.

You remove the barricades your ego has erected by putting your soul in charge. Your ego is a vital part of living on this Earth, but in order for you to obtain your goals of world peace you need to put your soul in charge of your life, not your ego.

Your life was meant to be enjoyed. It is much easier to enjoy your life when your soul is in charge. With your soul in charge, you have nothing to fear. With your soul in charge, you will always be working in the interests of your highest good, which is in the interests of All That Is. Your big Self will always be working towards world peace. Your big Self works towards unity. Your ego works towards separation.

❈❈❈

Love Lessons

You know that Jesus was very highly evolved when he appeared as a human on your planet. There are very few humans who obtain such high states of evolution. Yet, sooner or later, you all will get to the stage where you can walk on water, make the blind to see and the deaf to hear, and raise the dead. These are all examples of expressions of love and faith. Love and faith are the key elements in achieving all of your aims.

Everyone is in a different stage of development. Everyone had lessons in the spiritual realm before incarnating into the physical realm. You come to the physical realm to practise what you learned in spirit, but also there are more lessons for you here, more lessons of love, as well as practising what you learned and already know.

Even though you had lessons in spirit and your soul already knows everything you need to know in this lifetime, you cannot use that information without taking it into your physical brain. As we mentioned in your previous book, you receive information by way of books, videos, other people, all sorts of ways you receive information that you know about, and directly into your brain, as we mentioned in your previous book, from teachers in the spirit realm or Ascended Masters' realm.

All of life is filled with lessons if you believe it so. All of life is about love, so all of your lessons are about love, even though they may be given other names, like forgiveness, maintaining peace, sharing, etc.

Even though you may have one main lesson to learn in this lifetime, one main aspect of divinity you wish to practise expressing, there are other lessons included in your life. This is why you agree to come back to new lifetimes: you wish to experience yourself as divine, but also it is interesting and exciting for you when viewed from the perspective of the spirit realm.

From your more limited perspective of the physical realm, many of you find the lessons daunting, perhaps painful. But as you progress in your development, you learn tools to help you cope with the pain, and to overcome the challenges which your lessons present you with. You may still suffer, but only if you forget your lessons, and this is then good practice for you in adapting your lessons.

Even Jesus had some setbacks during his time on Earth, but he remembered his lessons and moved past those setbacks to become an example to you all. And remember, you are all examples to someone.

Think of yourselves as Jesus' brothers and sisters. Even though Jesus provided examples for all his siblings, each of you has something you can teach some of your siblings. I know you are all doing the best you can, but if you remember that you, too, are an example to others, you may just make that extra effort to step up—to be even better.

Know however, that no matter what you do and however many times you fail in applying your lessons or fail to be the best example that you yourself would wish to be, you can never disappoint me. I love you all unconditionally. I love you regardless of anything you may think, say, or do, or anything you may not think, say, or do.

Know that Jesus loves you unconditionally as well.

He is a beacon to all the world. Each of you is aiming to apply your lessons, which will lead you to become unconditionally loving to all. However, as each of you learns to be unconditionally loving, you can still be a beacon to each other, shining your light and love out into the world for all to see.

You are the light of the world, and I love you all.

Visitors from Other Planets

Love creates worlds and universes. You know about the part of the universe that you can see by means of the naked eye, telescopes and spaceships. What you may not be aware of is the vast expanse that is the universe and all the myriad of planets, stars, and all manner of celestial bodies imaginable. In some of those dwell other life forms. Some are similar to your own and some are so far removed from any life form familiar to you that you wouldn't recognise it as life.

Even on your planet, you don't recognise life as I know it to be. Because God created everything in the universe from God, and God is life, everything in the universe is alive, that is filled with life.

But on other planets and other celestial bodies, there are such life forms that even your Star Wars *writers would be surprised. At this time, some of these life forms are waiting to help the planet Earth in its transition. Some of the life forms are human-like; others are very different. All of these are more evolved than Earth's humans and are keen to help you with your transition to the world of your dreams. They are merely waiting until love has become more prominent in your thoughts before they introduce themselves to you.*

If they were to introduce themselves to you now, you may use your weapons to harm them. They have some protection from your weapons, being more advanced beings, but they wish to wait until it is safe for all concerned before offering assistance.

But to whom would they offer their assistance?

Your movies would have them getting in touch with an American scientist, or perhaps the President of the USA. But more likely, they would come in disguise, perhaps present themselves as Earthly humans. Rather than offering their services to people who control the purse strings of wealthy nations, chances are, they would offer their services to those who could control the heart strings.

They may come to you if you are a healer or spiritual leader. They may come to Joe Bloggs up the road, who runs the local family-owned grocery store. They may visit the Dalai Lama, or perhaps the Pope. Expect the unexpected.

You may ask if this could possibly be happening. Why would these beings from other planets visit with people who cannot make a difference in the world?

It is because every one of you can make a difference.

You make a difference with your love, and you would make more of a difference with more love. These highly evolved beings will be able to teach you how to supercharge your love.

You can all change the world, given enough love. With love and faith, you can move mountains. These highly evolved beings from other worlds will be in a position to train all of those who wish to learn how to use their love and faith to create the world you wish to see, and once created, how to maintain it and help it evolve even further.

The evolution of the Earth is on the threshold. You are on the threshold of doing great things, and with help from these highly evolved beings, even greater things are possible.

Life on your planet will begin to evolve even faster around the world. There will be no stopping it.

But it starts with you, with the love that dwells within you.

Who can you share your love with today?

Who can you share your love with tomorrow?

Changing Form

Now that you know where to start, don't ask when it will end, for evolution never ends. Your evolution is eternal.

Talking in celestial terms, you know that some stars explode and some implode. Physical matter may be strewn across the universe. As you know from your science classes, matter cannot be created or destroyed. It just changes form. Some changes form into a different type of matter. Some changes into energy, perhaps later to change back into matter again. But all of my creation is eternal. You are eternal.

You know that you are born into your physical body, but you also have a mind and a soul. You are a three-part being. At the time of your physical death, those parts of you which emanated from the Earth return to the Earth; those parts of you from the mind of God return to the mind of God; and those parts of you from the spirit realm return to the spirit realm.

Once your spirit has returned to that realm, you have the chance of further evolution in a number of different ways, including further lessons designed to prepare you for your next sojourn to Earth. You could, however, choose a different adventure in an entirely different part of the universe.

Time and space are linked, so you may decide to go back in time or forward in time, or to a different place in space. You could travel to a different spiritual realm for a totally different experience and lessons preparing you for totally different experiences elsewhere.

But you are the creator of your life, both the physical life you are in now, and all of your other physical lives. The spiritual part of you knows exactly what it will be doing next, but it can change its mind—you can change your mind at any time.

But what mind? Didn't you say your mind returns to God?

Your mind on Earth is made up of your ego mind and your God mind. That part of you which is your God mind returns to God. That part of you which is your ego mind returns to your spirit, to be used as and when it desires.

Most people in spirit only need to re-establish their ego mind when they come back to visit a loved one on the physical plane. The ego is what identifies you to your loved one. Without that, they would not recognise your energy.

As you can see, it is a very complex business, but you don't need to know all of what goes on after your physical death, because you would have trouble understanding from your limited perspective. But suffice to say: the choices are vast and your evolution is eternal.

May I ask a question now, God?

Yes, Lorelle.

You said that the God mind returns to God and the ego mind is put on a shelf, so to speak. How do we think in spirit? We had a discussion about the ramifications of thought on the spirit plane. I can't remember the exact words, but you gave the impression that thought happened in spirit. So how do we think, if you have taken back your God mind?

It is not so much taken back as melded into one. In spirit, you become one with God. Your spirit then separates from God to a certain extent, sufficient to be able to make individual decisions, but still connected to the God mind by energetic links.

If the soul or spirit can still make individual choices, does it not need an individual mind?

No, thought in spirit is an entirely different thing. The word 'thought' doesn't cover the process involved, but it is the only thing you understand from your physical perspective.

If we always have a spiritual part to us, why can't we use our spiritual 'thought' process in our physical lives?

You do. Your soul is choosing using this 'thought' process every second of every day. The link between the mind that you know of, which is more associated with your physical life, and the 'thought' process associated with your soul is a complicated one Lorelle. Suffice to say that you are often in two minds on Earth, whereas in spirit you are a singular being with a singular thought process.

The Joy of Service

Now, Lorelle, we had quite an in-depth serious discussion last night, so tonight I'd like to talk about something more fun. I wanted to talk about your life in the New Spirituality. We have talked about sex, and people from other planets visiting you on Earth.

Now I wanted to talk about your society, and what your communities might be like.

You know you have free will to do whatever you wish, so this is just a suggestion of what you might to do, once the world has changed to a more peaceful place and love has overtaken the world.

There will be more joy, as we mentioned in your previous book. You know that to bring out the joy in yourself, you just need to bring out the joy in another. It will be a joy to be of service to others. This includes animals, plants, and Mother Earth, along with all that makes up her great expanse.

As you know, animal communication and other telepathic communication will be much more widespread in the New Spirituality. Now, many people try to do the right thing by animals but fail to take into account the individual animal's opinions. In the New Spirituality, most people will have no trouble communicating with animals and learning their wishes. Whereas before, they may have separated families or communities, in the New Spirituality people will learn that animals have communities much like humans, as was pointed out in your study of the Koran. It will therefore be much easier to be of true service to animals, rather than just aiming to be of service.

This will be particularly important at the time nearing an animal's physical death. Many humans now suffer greatly because they believe they have to end the physical suffering of an animal by euthanasia, which is practised much less with humans. You know that sometimes a human needs to prepare for their death, along with their families, and the same applies to some companion animals. Once you can all find out the true wishes of your companion animals, you will know when to intervene to end suffering, if at all. Also, knowing that animals' souls too choose the timing of their own physical deaths, you can know that you have nothing to feel guilty about.

You wonder how this can be possible, if the animal's guardian is the one who chooses when to end the animal's suffering. Your human soul and your animal's soul are in communication. Yes, sometimes there are two or more people having different opinions on the timing of the intervention, and this means that there is a possibility that the animal's soul has had to make a compromise in relation to the timing. This is where the communication skill will be very important. Whereas now, although the soul of the animal chooses to compromise on its preferred timing, in the future, it will be able to make its choices known to you. In either case, it still happens in accordance with the animal's wishes.

You see, there is much going on behind the scenes that you don't know about, a collaboration of sorts between souls. Whereas you in the physical realm may feel like you are left in the dark, so to speak, in the spiritual realm, everything is illuminated; all is clear. You, Lorelle, have sometimes said you feel like you are Truman in The Truman Show, *with spiritual beings making decisions and manipulating your reality to achieve certain aims. The truth is not really so much different from this, but far more complex.*

But I digress.

We were talking about how wonderful it will be in the New Spirituality, because everyone will be of service to others. Your telepathic abilities will just make it easier to do that well.

So what would you like to do in the New Spirituality? The fact is you may not be doing anything very much different from what you are doing today. You may just be doing it more consciously, more aware of the consequences of all that you do, and aiming to make all of the consequences of your thoughts, words, and deeds in keeping with the highest good of All That Is.

You will find much joy in your employment, just because of this one aspect. You will also find more joy because you will be much more aware of the joy you are bringing to others, thus bringing out more joy in yourself. In the New Spirituality, you will be much more aware of all the consequences of your actions. Let's look at some examples.

Say you are an artist who paints landscapes. In the New Spirituality, you will have a greater understanding of the joy your paintings bring to others, and thus find even more joy in your work. As a chambermaid making beds and tidying hotel rooms, you will be much more aware of the appreciation your customers feel as they notice their clean surroundings and get to sleep in a comfortable bed.

So, you see, you may not do anything different; you may just do it differently, knowing that the more joy you bring to others, the more you bring to yourself. You may then try even harder to provide the service that you have always provided, and will enjoy it even more.

Your leisure time will be equally more joyful. Chances are you will spend less time on your electronic devices and more time interacting with real people, but if you do communicate with people electronically, you will have the added bonus of being able to communicate with them telepathically as well.

You know, you may even get to be so evolved that you can teleport yourselves using only the power of your minds, but that might take a while to achieve. In the meantime, your scientists and engineers may develop devices which can help you to teleport your body. Prior to that, you may just teleport yourselves virtually, as such technology is nearly available now.

There will be many such advances coming along, but whereas your previous technological advances may have been developed with little regard for the consequences, future advances will always consider the consequences to All That Is.

This may be difficult in the transition period, because you may not have yet developed the telepathic skills to ensure that the consequences to individuals are always positive. But remember that you can always think love before everything you think, say and do, and then you are more likely to cause only positive consequences.

There may be times when you think that what you are doing will have detrimental consequences, even after thinking love. On those occasions, it would be best to meditate on the issue, and ask your spiritual helpers for clarity on the matter. However, you may not fully understand the consequences for All That Is, so it is best to follow your feelings, which are the voice of your soul, after first thinking love. But remember that your spiritual helpers will always be available to help you.

❄❄❄

Expressing Love

Even though we all are made of love, it is the expression of love which allows you to experience your love. You can express love for yourself, which we said is the first step in being able to express your love to others, because until you feel your love you can't share it with others. You can share an idea of love, but not actual love. But if you can think love for yourself first, it is then easier to think love for others. As Jesus said, you need to love one another as yourself.

So how do you learn to express your love? It is easy. You just have to remove the blocks you have placed, which are stopping the expression of your love. As we mentioned before, you may need help to remove these blockages. Your parents and society have taught you that you shouldn't love yourself, only others, but it is vital to love yourself first. And when you tried to love others physically, they frowned upon that as well.

It is becoming much easier in today's society to love others physically, but there is still a stigma around it. For instance, how much love are you allowed to show in public? Some societies frown upon kissing and hugging in public. Even feeding babies in public is frowned upon by some, condemning a very innocent form of love.

There are a lot of learned behaviours and learned beliefs in your societies, which are holding you back from full and free expression of your love. But how much love should you be allowed to express in public?

This is a difficult question, Lorelle, because if loving an individual in public is causing upset to another individual, is it then in the highest good of All That Is, because isn't that upset person just as much a part of All That Is as the individual you wish to express love to?

When you start to learn to follow your feelings, you realise that what may be appropriate in one society, may not be appropriate in another. What may be appropriate in one moment, may not be appropriate in the next.

Even once you learn to follow your feelings, you may still make mistakes. Perhaps you just forgot to consider your feelings and forgot to think love before your actions. But there are no such things as mistakes in God's world. Even those things which you may decide you would have done differently if you had your time over again, even those things will all end up being for the highest good of All That Is.

The universe is created in such a way that even your perceived mistakes end up changing the world for the better. Everything ends up having a positive effect in the end, even those things which seem to have a negative effect in the short term.

What is God?

You may be wondering if there is anything more we could write about love. We could fill volumes, and still not run out. For, as you know, everything is made of love—every grain of sand, every heavenly body, and everything in between. Imagine the stories we could tell about all those things.

Everything is evolving. Everything is changing.

The sand is being worn down, and it is also being built up into rocks. The heavenly bodies collide and explode and build outwards from molten cores. Plants grow and decay. Humans are born, have children and die.

But no one dies. Nothing is ever really destroyed. God is an infinite being who has divided itself into an infinite number of parts to create the universe.

All of those infinite number of parts are combining and breaking apart, becoming compounds, breaking apart into elements, becoming energy and matter, but always the whole of the parts are still there, no matter how many ways and times they change, adapt, merge, blend, and erode.

But we are all one. One God. One universe. One creation.

You are a child of God, created in the spiritual image of God, not the physical image of God.

God did not begat God, and yet God did, because God is everything. God is everything that begat and everything that was begotten.

You cannot contain God. God is ever expanding, but God is also ever contracting. God is an expanding universe and a contracting universe. God is all light, but God is also black holes.

So what is God? God is all there is. God is love. Love is all there is. God is you. You are God.

We are one.

Being God has its responsibilities. As God, you need to allow free will to be paramount. God cannot impel anyone to do anything, yet God must support and allow everyone to do everything.

But if you are God, do you have these same responsibilities? Only if you know you are God. If you know you are God, then you must act as God.

But God can't impel you to do anything. So God cannot impel you as God to act as God.

You see the dilemma? This is why I have given you angels—to help you act as God without impelling you. This is how I have supported you. I have sent you nothing but angels.

God is an impartial witness to all that you do, a witness who experiences all that you experience. So how can God be impartial, if God experiences the same things as you?

You can never fully understand all that God is from your limited perspective in the physical realm. Even in the spiritual realm, you cannot fully grasp what God is. Even the angels who are closest to God cannot fully grasp all that God is.

When God separated itself into parts such as humans and angels, it knew that no single part of God could ever understand the enormity of God.

Yet, as Lorelle discovered, you can come close to merging with God even in your physical realm. As you come close to merging with God, you come closer to a full comprehension, but still can never fully understand God.

When you leave your physical body behind, you merge with God for a short while if you wish, but even here, you keep a certain amount of separation, sufficient to keep you as an individual being within the vast expanse of God. As in one analogy we have used, it is as a wave in the ocean.

There is much about life that you will never know, even about life on your planet. But imagine all of the millions of wonderful things there are to learn about life. And as you know, life is just another name for God.

You are here to learn about love. You are here to learn about yourself. You are here to learn about God.

Would you like more lessons about love? Just look outside your door. Pick something and study it. Look at your child or your pet. Examine a drop of water or a snowflake, a leaf, or a grain of sand.

❄❄❄

The Tools for Overcoming Suffering

I love you, Lorelle, and all of my creation, but I know that many of you suffer. As my children, I do not wish any of you to suffer. Yet you do.

Lorelle learned some lessons about reducing your suffering in this life, which she shared in her previous book. The first lesson was to think love before all that you do. The second lesson was to live in the moment. The third lesson was to follow your feelings—to move towards those feelings which bring you joy and away from those feelings which bring you discomfort.

This last lesson is difficult if you have not yet learned to listen to the voice of your higher self and have not yet learned that your higher self speaks through the feelings in your body.

The problem here is that sometimes your ego hijacks your communication between your higher self and your body and causes blockages. It puts a barrier up on the railway tracks, stopping the train of communication from your higher self getting through to your body. It hijacks your body with fear.

When your ego has presented your body with fear, it goes into the fight, flight or freeze reaction. This reaction takes all of your attention, as it is a means of survival when faced with a sabre-tooth tiger or a ferocious bear. Your body knows it needs to escape this fear by one of these three methods until the danger is passed.

The problem is that the fear your ego creates is unfounded on any real threat to your body. The threat it creates is really a threat to your mind, to your ego. Your ego usually has you frightened of what might happen if... Fill in the blank with what it is your ego mind has been frightened of recently. You all have an ego, so you all have scenarios that your ego mind imagines could happen, which cause you fear if you listen to it.

Usually, these fears are only a problem if you forget to live in the moment, and why living in the moment is a very important lesson. It is often accompanied by your forgetting to think love. Because if you had thought love first, chances are you would not be listening to your ego voice, but rather the voice of your higher self.

When you start listening to your ego voice instead of your higher self's voice, your body is only feeling fear and not the feelings that are coming from your higher self. If you are not yet accustomed to the difference, you may mistake the feelings of your body and continue to move away from the fearful feeling towards your comfort zone.

Your ego creates this space where it won't feel threatened—for a while at least. If you continue to listen to your ego voice, it will continue to feel threatened by something, because it is not happy unless it is keeping you in fear.

However, if you continue to follow the voice of your ego, you will be moving further and further away from the voice of your higher self, which would lead you to joy.

This is the reason most of you suffer: you are listening to the wrong voice.

If you wish to feel joy more often, it is important to follow these three steps: think love, live in the moment, and follow your feelings after that.

Most of you manage to live in the moment at least for part of your day, so most of you can remain at least a little bit joyful at times throughout your day. When you find yourself never following these three steps because you are always listening to your ego, this is when you risk spiralling into depression. As Lorelle can attest from her experience with family members, once you get a long way down this spiral, it is very hard to climb back up. And once your ego has shown you the route down that spiral, it likes to lead you there as often as possible.

Thinking love is a simple and quick way to help you start the climb back up.

Many of you lead stressful lives. Stress usually only occurs because you don't follow these three steps. But when you allow stress to build up in your body, it is important to release it, because too much stress will have you back into that fight, flight or freeze response again.

One way of releasing stress is through regular meditation. Meditation allows you to get in touch with your higher self, which reminds you that there is nothing to fear in this moment.

There are other ways of releasing stress and all of them lead you to the present moment. In the present moment, there is nothing to stress about.

Stress is just a way for your ego to keep you in fear and is caused by you worrying about the future or thinking about the past and worrying that something that happened in the past could happen again, or worrying about why something that you hoped would happen didn't happen or why something happened that you hoped wouldn't. Stress is caused by not living in the moment. In the present moment, there is nothing to fear and nothing to stress about.

The present moment is where God resides. The present

moment is where you will find joy.

Now that you know how to stay in joy and rid yourself of stress and suffering, I'm sure you will want to ensure you follow these three steps as much as possible.

You may need to practise them, so you may find that your spiritual helpers will provide you with scenarios which provide this practice. Even though those scenarios may be less than pleasant, you can ask your spiritual helpers to only give you practice that you will enjoy, or at least are not too painful. The more you practise, the better you will cope with more difficult scenarios which may present themselves in your life.

You may start asking the question: "What is wrong with my comfort zone? I like it here." Your comfort zone is only comfortable while you live in the moment. Your comfort zone becomes uncomfortable if you start listening to your ego voice, which will have you living in fear.

This is how agoraphobia develops. If anxiety presents itself when you walk out the door, it is more comfortable to stay inside. But then your ego tells you that you don't really want to stay inside, so you become anxious about not being able to go out. Left untreated, you become anxious about everything. Maybe the phone will ring, and you'll have to speak to someone. Maybe someone will come to the door. According to your ego, threats are everywhere. If you listen to your ego for too long, you're back in bed, at the bottom of that depression spiral once again.

Think love; live in the moment; follow your feelings; get out of bed. Think love; live in the moment; follow your feelings; get dressed and step out the door—and so it goes on.

You may have setbacks, but only if you are listening to your ego voice.

The Ego Creates Conflict

As well as creating depression, the ego creates conflict because it likes to keep you separate from God and everybody else. We are one, as you know, but if we are one, the ego is concerned that it will disappear. Its identity, your ego identity, is based on you being an individual, separate from all others.

Your soul would see you love everyone unconditionally. Your ego would see you separated from everyone.

So how do you reconcile these two voices in your head? You need to trust the inner guidance that is the voice of your higher self. This is the voice of love.

The fact is that any conflict between you and another is a reflection of the conflict in your mind. When you allow your higher self to control your mind, you love your ego and all others, realising that we are one. When you allow your ego to control your mind, you see yourself as separate from others.

The real conflict is in your mind. Rather than being afraid of the other, it is really God that you are afraid of. God would see you become one with God. Your ego fears this as it fears its death, the loss of self. It fights against the God part of you, and in so doing fights against others as well.

To keep itself separate, the ego has to create someone who is the other. You will notice that sometimes people can love their family, but not anyone outside their family. Sometimes they can love the people of their own community, but not anyone outside their community. Sometimes they can love anyone who belongs to their religion, but not anyone outside their religion. Sometimes the other they create is anyone from another country.

The separation, this differentness that is created, is an illusion, because we are one.

Sometimes people accept and love other humans but separate themselves from other parts of God's creation—Mother Earth, the animals, the natural world.

This separation is an illusion. We are all one.

So how do we solve the conflicts created by the ego?

We revert back to our lessons. Firstly, think love in relation to yourself, including your ego. It is then easier to think love towards the other. Knowing it is loved, the ego is not so much on the defensive.

"But," I hear you say, "they started it."

We can always find an excuse to continue a conflict that has already started. "It's not my fault." But if you consider that we are all one, it was you who started it, because I and you are one. So what is the answer?

Love.

Ask: "What would love do now?"

There are two sides to every conflict. If they started it, they had a reason. Yes, we know that it was their ego that wished to create separation, but even so they needed to find an excuse to create this conflict, even if the conflict is based on an illusion. Understanding their reason for the conflict is the key to ending the conflict. Throw enough love at any situation and it will be resolved positively.

When someone is acting from their ego, often, there is no arguing with them. You cannot get them to understand what is right, but it is your ego which has a need to be right. Your higher self doesn't need to be right. Your higher self allows love to be right. Love may just walk away from a conflict. Love may aim to help, change the subject, point out positives for the other party. Love may compromise. The solution may be different for each conflict, but the underlying solution is love.

So how do you stop your ego from causing conflict?

Think love. But when you operate from the ego, you don't think love; you think separation. So, often it is only in hindsight that you can look at a situation that has led to conflict and see that it was your ego that was reacting to the other. In a personal conflict, it is often because the other person has said or done something which feels like an attack to your ego.

If, for example, your ego thinks of itself as a good husband, and someone tells you you're a bad husband, your ego perceives an attack. It is an attack on your identity which is linked to your ability as a husband. Each person is different and has different buttons which cause the ego to react, thus taking you further away from the voice of your higher self towards the voice of your ego. If you are listening to your ego, your higher self can't get a word in. This is why you may not end up being aware of the fact that your ego was engaged until after the fact.

If you have been involved in a conflict and you later analyse the reasons for it, you will see that you allowed your ego to take charge. The more you realise what happened, the easier it will be, if a similar situation happens again, to remember what triggered your ego to feel attacked and which of your buttons were pressed. If you are aware of your buttons, you can realise when your ego feels attacked and you can instantly give it love, before it starts to take charge. You can reassure it that it is loved and not really under attack. The attack is an illusion. Once your higher self has gained control and you have given love to yourself including your ego, you can send love to the 'other', thus calming the situation.

Each time you recognise your buttons are pressed, you can reassure your ego, and practise responding with love instead of conflict.

Love takes practice, and your ego is a wonderful tool given you by your creator to allow you to get plenty of practice. You don't need to reprimand your ego for reacting with conflict. You can thank it and love it for providing you with a means to practise being love.

❅❅❅

Jesus

Lorelle, what would you like to talk about tonight?

You've managed pretty well without much input from me. Why not carry on?

No, Lorelle, we want to make this a joint venture, so what would you like to talk about?

Something has popped into my mind. It was Jesus, but I know we talked about Jesus in WE ARE ONE.

Yes, Lorelle, we have talked about Jesus before, but I'm sure he won't mind if we talk about him again.

You are right that he performed many miracles and a lot of what he achieved was not recorded. It is a bit like your modern news media, which only reports things they think people will be interested in. The smaller miracles, like your computer mouse being fixed, get overlooked. Jesus cured people of illnesses, but he also created miracles in his dealings with people. He used love to bring people together; some turned from enemies to friends. He did things like walk on water, not to show off how advanced he was compared to others, but he told them that these sorts of things they could do themselves, given sufficient faith. He used his love to achieve marvellous things.

His greatest achievement was his crucifixion and resurrection. You know that he was a gifted man who could have used his gifts to escape crucifixion, but he chose to give his life so that others may live. He gave his physical life, so that others would know that life is eternal. Even though he knew that his life is eternal, as is everyone's, it was still a great sacrifice to give himself for crucifixion, not because he would lose his life, because he knew he is eternal, but still it was a traumatic and courageous way to die.

I know that many of you have asked to die peacefully in your sleep, and Jesus could have asked this too, and his desire would have been granted to him, just as yours are, but he chose to offer himself in this way knowing it would be a difficult passing. Because he was very advanced in his development, he was able to separate his consciousness from his body early on, so as not to suffer as much as others might have during crucifixion, but it was still a brave thing to do. And he did it for you, for you all, so that you would all know that life is eternal.

Couldn't he have chosen an easier death and still shown that life is eternal?

Not really, Lorelle. He was a public figure by the time of his death, and to achieve his aims he needed to have a public death, so that everyone who saw him on the cross became a witness to his death, so his resurrection was so much more remarkable.

❄︎❄︎❄︎

Hate

Lorelle, today we wanted to talk about love again. I know that you don't know all about love yet, because we discussed that love is everything, and you don't know everything about everything. So there is much to learn.

Today we want to talk about hate, and how that is a form of love, and how we can combat, for want of a better word, hate with love.

You just thought of a quote from Martin Luther King Jr.

"Darkness cannot drive out darkness; only light can do that.

Hate cannot drive out hate; only love can do that."

And he was right; you can only drive out hate with love.

But as you know, hate is just another form of love. The question you need to ask yourself is: why do people hate? It is usually a form of love for someone, even if only for oneself.

Why did the Nazis hate the Jews? Because they had been told that the Jews were the cause of all their problems. So they hated, because they loved themselves. Hate, however, is another form of listening to the ego. So even though hate is caused by loving themselves, it doesn't include love for all, as your higher self would have you do. Hate is driven by the ego.

While we are on the subject of the treatment of the Jews by the Nazis and Hitler, I know that there were, and still are, people who say that there can't be a God, because a God would never let that happen. God would never allow millions of people to be killed in such a way. But, as we discussed, free will is paramount. God cannot interfere in the free will of any of God's creation.

But God, you have said to me that, if I ask you for anything, it is mine as surely as night follows day. I am sure you meant this as a general statement to all humanity, and I'm sure that lots of people asked you to help the Jews and all the other people oppressed by the Nazis. Was it not the will of those millions that they would be saved?

They were saved, Lorelle, just not in the physical sense. As you know, friendly souls agree to be the victim in such scenarios, so that they and others can experience those things they came to Earth to experience. Even though it is hard to imagine from your physical perspective, all of those souls incarnated in that lifetime knowing that that would be the way they would leave their physical lives.

It is difficult to imagine. Did not the will of those Jews really desire to live in their physical bodies?

Even though I mentioned to you that you will always choose the timing and method of transition, it may not always be consciously. Sometimes it is in the interests of your soul to keep you 'in the dark', so to speak, especially if you are not meditating regularly and staying in touch with your higher self.

I know this is hard to hear for many people, but as we mentioned, the situation looks so much different from the spiritual realm. Those people who were able to give that physical life for others received much joy from the experience. Those people who were the instigators of what you would call atrocities received valuable spiritual lessons in spirit from their experiences. They all received further lessons in aspects of divinity and went on to be able to experience what they learned while in spirit, after reincarnating. But as you know, all of this is happening now, sequentially but simultaneously.

As we mentioned in WE ARE ONE, Hitler has elected to stay in that merged state in order to recover from being the friendly soul to all those people who suffered.

Even though you may not understand it, every soul received something positive from the experience. Those people who were 'instigators' of the atrocities were acting as friendly souls to those who were the 'victims' of the atrocities, having colluded prior to incarnating to form a plan where the victims would learn to love themselves and their 'enemies', despite the way they were treated, and the 'instigators' were learning to forgive themselves following such atrocities.

Regardless of the spiritual lessons and the friendly souls' selfless actions, the scenarios which ensued are not necessarily as God would wish to see, for God in the form of Ultimate Reality only wishes to see love. However, the God of the physical world believes in free will for all and will not interfere with any such plans.

Your question regarding the prayers of the millions is difficult to answer. As you know, I promised you that, as night follows day, so your wish will be granted. Ask and you shall receive. Seek and you shall find. Knock and the door shall be opened unto you. Believe and it is so. But having said that, you create your own reality. Your will creates your reality, but your reality is affected by others' wills.

So, perhaps the question to ask God is not: "Why do bad things happen to good people?" but: "Why do good things happen to bad people?"

Self-confidence is a major factor, and what is another name for confidence, but faith? Those people who create the reality they desire more easily are those who have faith in their abilities and the universe's ability to bring them their desires.

But regardless of the actions and whether they are judged as good or bad, there are always consequences. As we mentioned in WE ARE ONE, there is no punishment by God, as some believe, but there is an equal and opposite reaction, which some call karma. This is the reason you are asked to do unto others as you would have them do unto you—because what goes around comes around. What you give out comes back to you.

But as Shakespeare wrote in Hamlet, *"There is nothing either good or bad, but thinking makes it so". There is only what serves you and what doesn't, given what you are trying to achieve. If what you are trying to achieve is a world where love rules and everyone is treated with respect, then what serves you is to make love the dominant force in your lives.*

Regarding your current view of those people involved in the actions of haters and their victims, the best course of action now would be to ask: "What would love do now?" Chances are, love would tell you that it would aim to forgive all those who caused suffering at that time and any time. Forgiveness is only necessary when you don't understand the reasons for the actions taken. Once you understand, you no longer need to forgive.

Because of the scale of the actions taken, and the way that history is portrayed to you, it is difficult for you to understand the reasons, which, hard as it may be for you to believe, were really about love—perhaps love for self, perhaps love for country, perhaps love for a leader. As it is difficult to understand, the best course of action is forgiveness.

It is much easier for you to understand when the situation does not have such a traumatic effect on your psyche. As empathic beings, you feel others' pain. Where there are a lot of people feeling pain, that pain encompasses those involved, those who hear about it, and those who are generations away from the actions. Love is the only way that the pain can be relieved. You all still suffer for this today, and each of you need to first love yourself in relation to this matter, and then send love to all those involved at the time, and all generations since, including your current one.

Love leads to forgiveness. Forgiveness leads to love.

Even though history teaches who was good and who was bad, that determination in some circumstances depends on your point of view.

❈ ❈ ❈

Ending Conflict in Palestine/Israel

Lorelle, I know that many years ago, you used to watch people in Israel and Palestine killing each other on the television and cry. You became determined never to visit Israel, or particularly Jerusalem, until peace reigns there. But do you think you could do anything to improve the situation there?

God, you know I don't keep up with current affairs these days, particularly conflict. I know there is still conflict, but I have no idea of the scale.

I know, Lorelle, but you could find out.

It became too painful for me to see the endless conflict there, but I could find out what the current situation is. I would love to be of help in resolving the situation there, but many have tried before me. I doubt there is anything I, as a nobody, could do to improve the situation, except send love.

Exactly, Lorelle, you could send them love, and you do, as you send your love out into the world, but you could send them love specifically to that area. You could ask for a solution to be found. You could ask for many people to pray for a solution. But you know that a prayer of gratitude is more likely to be successful.

"Thank you, God, for providing a peaceful solution to the conflict in Israel/Palestine and throughout the Middle East." If enough people offer this prayer, it is likely to be successful, but you know that everyone has free will. If the number of people holding expectations of solutions outweigh the number of people holding expectations of conflict, there is likely to be a positive outcome.

Love is the answer to all questions, and love can even end decades long conflicts.

Each person in those areas has had someone close to them who has been affected in some way by the decades of conflicts. Success is unlikely to happen overnight. It will take a lot of love being thrown at the area, but you can do it, if you join forces with all the others who wish for world peace.

Each person affected will need to remember the love that dwells within themselves, and to listen to the voice of the soul, which would tell them how to proceed. Their spiritual helpers can arrange counselling and meetings to discuss and listen to each others' grievances. For, only once the pain and suffering are acknowledged, can they be forgiven and released.

The first step is having the will to succeed in finding a peaceful solution, and in acknowledging that, for those people involved, the solution will come from within. Blaming someone else never brings a solution. It is important to understand the hurt that has been done to generations now of citizens there.

The pain and suffering of generations are cumulative. Layer upon layer of pain is built up until it is like an onion. In order to find a solution, we first have to peel off each layer of pain and apply love between each layer.

There are historical factors which add to the difficulties: the Holocaust, the British occupation, and other factors even before Israel existed, all adding to the psychological issues affecting the area.

It will take much determination and love to overcome these factors, but as each layer of pain is peeled away and love applied, new hope will arise. And the more hope, the more hope is possible, and soon more love will be applied and a solution will be found.

But someone has to make a start at a different solution than what has been tried before. I know you had previously thought that if people from both sides and all religions can sit down and talk, it would be a start. I know you wanted to include a panel or committee of people from the working classes in Israel/Palestine—those who would be affected by any change, and just get them to meet and talk and air their differences, and endeavour to find common ground. This could work if they start with the common ground of love and the intention of succeeding in finding a solution.

So where do we go from here?

Lorelle, you could start by learning about the current state of affairs. You could encourage a prayer vigil, explaining that prayers of gratitude are more efficient. You can send love to the area and encourage others to send love to the area. You can also ask for help from your spiritual helpers. Archangel Michael is able to help you with this if you ask.

I know, Lorelle, that you would be grateful to see peace in the Middle East. You will remember that it was watching a news story about fighting in the Middle East which caused you to offer your first prayer for world peace, and the reason you have worked so hard to help bring that about.

You would be very happy if you could visit Jerusalem, knowing that it is a peaceful place, open to all, with past horrors cleansed from its energy. It would once again become the sacred place it was destined to be.

Healing after Conflict

Lorelle, we were talking about bringing peace back to the Middle East, and Jerusalem in particular. But you know that, apart from the historical problems surrounding the origins of Israel and prior, there have also been problems in other parts of the Middle East, some of which we touched on in your previous book.

As you know, the West has been involved in trying to control and manipulate events in the Middle East for some time, often due to their wish to control oil supplies. However, in those countries where there has been colonial and other forces endeavouring to control the population, conflict and war have resulted. There is much hatred for the West in some people in some areas, due to western nations' efforts in the past, and in some instances present, to manipulate affairs in those countries.

If peace is ever going to reign throughout the world, there must be a meeting of people from all of those nations to air their grievances, and for those nations who were involved to acknowledge and seek forgiveness for their efforts at manipulation.

There are other countries other than western nations, which have endeavoured to manipulate events in other countries as well, such as China and Russia.

As you know, China and Korea sought acknowledgement and apologies from Japan for events which took place during World War II and just prior.

The point I am making, Lorelle, is it would be wrong to assume that once the ill feelings over events in the Middle East are healed, there will be no more global barriers to world peace. There are not only countries, but tribes and communities within countries, such as Rwanda and the United States where forgiveness for past hurts need to be sought.

Your planet has had a troubled history, and you all bear scars from the events of your time and your ancestors' times. The pain is cumulative in your genes and in the way you were raised; in other words, nurture and nature have their effects on you now.

All of these situations require love. You are helping by sending your love out into the world, but as we mentioned in relation to Israel, it is like an onion that needs to be peeled and love applied to each layer.

Once all the layers of pain are removed, you are not only providing healing in the present, but also helping to heal your ancestors in their current roles, wherever that may be.

Each nation needs to consider what it feels are still painful wounds and seek talks with the offending nations to provide acknowledgement of the grievances and forgiveness if possible. Forgiveness is always possible.

There is much to do before peace is likely to be achieved in every corner of the globe, but love is the answer. Once you apply love to any situation, it is healed. Because of the layers of pain, more love may be needed at a later time, but love will always conquer any problem and cure any ill.

Now that you know the work that is required, I don't want you to get discouraged. All of this will happen more quickly than you think, once a concerted effort is made by all to make love the dominant force in your country, and to apply love to past hurts caused by you and to you.

❄❄❄

The Lucifer Effect

We talked about the Middle East and other conflict zones, and the problems involved in mending bridges and allowing forgiveness in these areas. It is no coincidence that you happened to start reading the book you are reading: The Lucifer Effect[18] *by Philip Zimbardo, which details his experiment known as the Stanford Prison Experiment, but also talks about Rwanda and other trouble spots, other areas where horrible atrocities and genocide were enacted. I know you haven't read much of the book yet, but have you seen a common element yet, Lorelle?*

The common element so far has been that, in each of the cases, the perpetrators dehumanise the 'other' after first creating the 'other' out of people who, in many cases, were previously their former neighbours and friends.

It has been shocking to me to read. It seems that in the cases I have seen so far, an authority figure labels the victims as 'other' and blames them for their troubles. In killing the 'others', they feel they are ridding themselves of their troubles. I know there are other causes I am yet to read about.

Yes, Lorelle, the 'us' and 'them' situation is necessary to allow for 'us' to kill 'them'.

So, how do we overcome these traits in ourselves, because as the book points out, there is nothing 'evil' about these people, until they go on to enact evil acts?

Remembering the Golden Rule would help. If you do unto others as you would have them do unto you, you are unlikely to cause them harm, even if you have identified them as 'others'.

This is a basic tenet of all religions, so unless all of the people involved in such atrocious acts were people with no religion, it would seem that knowledge of this rule isn't enough. Instead, one would need to act with this rule in mind.

The problem is, Lorelle, that the authority figure overrides your internal guidance system, which should be your highest authority. If your authority figure gives you a new rule, your mind doesn't differentiate between the old rule, even if it is golden, and the new rule established by the authority figure.

As the book mentions, the problem is overcome only by those heroes who stand up against the authority and refuse to follow their rule. The problem is not only the authority figure who creates the rule, but the perpetrator's peers who add to the authority with threats of violence and peer pressure.

You saw from another experiment[19] what happens when people act in response to what others are doing, even if they don't know why they are doing it. In an optometrist's waiting room, everyone stood up for no apparent reason. The individual not privy to the study then stood up with the others, so as not to stand out.

No one wants to see themselves as different or become the 'other'. When there is the threat of death or worse for even being associated with the 'others', that is even greater incentive to go along with everyone else.

Regardless of the rules, do you think anyone could possibly carry out atrocities if you first think love?

No, Lorelle, you cannot. Again, love is the answer.

❊❊❊

Evil Is as Evil Does

Lorelle, you were going to tell me more of your thoughts on the book, The Lucifer Effect[20]*.*

Yes, God. It is at times disturbing, depressing, and enlightening.

It is disturbing because it demonstrates so many ways that a previously innocent person can be led to do evil things. It is depressing to know the depths to which normal people can go for no reason other than to cure boredom, or to follow orders. But more depressing because it is obvious that any one of us is capable of evil acts. We are all capable of avoiding evil and becoming heroes as well, as those who didn't succumb were called. Overall, I found the book shows that there are no evil people, only evil situations and evil systems which provide an environment for ordinary people to carry out evil acts.

There are also so many psychological systems which help to lead us towards evil acts that it seems a wonder there are so few of such acts. However, the chief cause, as I mentioned before, seemed to be creating an 'us' and a 'them'—calling someone else the 'other'. The 'others' were the Jews in Germany or the Tutsis in Rwanda, or the prisoners or the guards in the Stanford Prison Experiment.

It became obvious to me that if we are all capable of evil, we have no basis for categorising anyone as better or worse than us.

Your soul and the grace of God can keep you from doing evil deeds, but only if you are listening to your soul. As we have mentioned, the best way to ensure a positive outcome for All That Is is to think love before all that you think, say, and do, and to listen to your feelings, which are the voice of your soul, the closest part of you to God. Your soul will likely have you acting in accordance with the highest good of All That Is.

You are right that aspects of this study are disturbing and depressing, because you could easily see yourself succumbing to the influences described in the book. As the book told you, most people could never imagine a situation where they would end up doing those evil things mentioned, and yet the book provides so much evidence that virtually every person is susceptible.

So what can you do?

You can think love before all that you think, say, and do, you can also be aware. You can be conscious. You can be conscious of the fact that you are just as susceptible as anyone else. You can be conscious of the fact that creating any other being as an 'other', who is in some way not deserving of the same respect as yourself, could lead you to evil thoughts, words, and deeds. You can follow Jesus' example of loving your neighbour as yourself. Remember, too, his example of standing up to others who he saw about to stone a woman, and asking that he who is without sin could cast the first stone. I would go further to suggest that he who is incapable of sin could cast a stone, because as you discovered in this book, there is none among you incapable of sin.

Where We Are Heading

Lorelle, tonight I wanted to talk about where we are heading. I know we discussed all this in WE ARE ONE[21], *but you know it depends a lot on the way humans treat the planet, and how quickly they can change their ways of thinking, speaking, and acting to be based on love. Many of you, if not most of you, do use love in your thoughts, words, and actions from time to time, but there are very few, if any, who use love throughout their day.*

I know it takes practice to remember to think love before all that you think, say, and do, but even after practice, you still forget. Once you forget to think love and your ego takes over control, things tend to go from bad to worse, and then you are so far removed from your true self, from your higher self, that it can be hard to come back from that.

This is one of the reasons that counting to ten when you get angry can be a good idea. Anger is a natural reaction and it is best to express it, but counting to ten gives you time to consider how you want to express your anger. Rather than lashing out at your partner, for instance, you might think to go for a walk and let out your anger at the sky, or perhaps pound a pillow.

You are all doing the best you can, but you each have free will to do things which can help you to react better each time. For instance, meditating and regular exercise help to relieve stress, which is a major cause of poor reactions—of less than loving reactions to a situation.

Are you doing all that you can as an individual to help bring about the world of your desires?

God, I know that I often think I could do better or do more, but find I haven't a lot of time for the things I think of. I know most of us in today's society feel like we have more and more things to do, and less and less time to do it. I am retired, but still have lots of things to do that don't get done.

I know, Lorelle, that you all lead busy lives, but it is necessary to prioritise those things you see as important, if you want to make important changes. Turn off the TV, put down that book, put your work on improving the lot of the world higher up your priority list.

Often, too, we don't know the best course of action at any given time.

I know, because you forget to ask for help from your spiritual helpers. Asking: "What would love do now?" would help.

So what happens now in relation to improving things on your planet depends on each of you prioritising improving things on your planet.

There are a lot of things each of you can do. You can buy organic, vegan, and cruelty free products, which do not cause harm to animals or the environment. You can pick up rubbish where you see it. You can opt for cleaning products and packaging which are not detrimental to the environment. You can install solar panels or wind turbines to produce electricity. You can send peace, love and healing out into the world, and you can consider the consequences to the planet of everything you think, say, and do.

You can make love the dominant force in your life by thinking love before all that you think, say, and do, and you can ask "What would love do now?" when faced with a decision.

Now that you know what you need to do to move forward towards the world of your dreams, you will want others to help you. You may be tempted to coerce others to do something they don't really want to do. The best way to lead others is by example. The best way to see more love take over the world is to first share your love with others. Remember that the more you give, the more you get. So in giving love, you get love.

There are many ways you can share love with the world. Each of you has an individual role to play. For some, it is writing a book. Others develop new products which are better for the environment. Others create videos which bring information to people about ways they can help. Each of you has a role to play. But there are other things that all of you can do to help.

Sending your love out into the world is one important way. Thinking love before all you do is another. There are many ways to bring more love into the world. Consider smiling at others instead of frowning. Consider complimenting others and offering them appreciation for just being themselves or for something they have done. Consider telling your loved ones how much you love them, even more than you do now. Consider showing them how much you love them by hugs and kisses, doing small acts of kindness, helping with chores, small gifts.

There are lots of ways to bring more love into the world. You just need to make love the dominant force in your lives.

❄❄❄

God's Preferred Name

God, as you know, I sent an email to my newsletter recipients telling them that, if they wanted to submit a question, I would take one question to submit to you for an answer, even though everyone is quite capable of asking God a question for themselves.

The person phrased it slightly differently, but the question revolved around the fact that there are so many names for God, and the word 'God', has certain connotations which some people react to. With so many names for you, God, such as Universe, Source, All That Is, plus all foreign language names, is there a name that you prefer to be called?

It is as you were just thinking, Lorelle, my preferred name is Love. Love is a different word in different languages, so it would be different depending on what language you speak.

Some of my older names have outlived their usefulness. They are often associated with a God of punishment and, as we discussed previously, God does not punish, merely allows the universe to create equal and opposite reactions for any thought, word, or deed. But also, as you know, with God all things are possible, so it is possible to change the consequences given sufficient love and faith.

Anyway, regarding God's name, as your reader suggested, God has been known by so many names, and like anything humans do, God has no opinion on the matter. God merely advises the best course of action, given the outcome you wish to achieve. As you are all working towards the outcome of a more positive planet, where love rules, peace reigns, and everyone is treated with respect, the best course of action would be to use the name for God which brings the most love into the world. Love would do that, but if you wish to differentiate the name for God, the creator, from the name for God's creation, then love may be a bit confusing, because love is what you all are.

I would therefore suggest that you call me the name that makes you think of love when you hear it. If any of my old names has the opposite effect, then it is not helping to move you towards your goals.

The Lessons

When I was creating my previous books, I was in the midst of some painful experiences, including spiritual lessons which I related to my readers in the hopes of helping them avoid the painful experiences which I had endured. Creating this book, however, was a joy to me. Nevertheless, there are still lessons to be learned from it.

I have summarised some of those lessons below:

You can communicate with your higher self and spiritual helpers on awakening and during meditation, when the ego voice is quiet. Your angels and other spiritual helpers are always available to ask for help. Everyone can learn to communicate telepathically with angels, other spiritual beings, animals and other humans. When communicating with spiritual beings, it is best to surround yourself in white light and ask to communicate with angels and/or high-vibrational guides only.

Archangels and all angels are genderless, but can present themselves to us as masculine or feminine, depending on their role. We now have other archangels, known as archaiai, who present themselves as feminine, in order to bring a balance back to the Earth, away from the imbalance of our patriarchal societies.

Love is all there is. Love creates everything, including war and hatred. However, usually this is only love of oneself, one's family, one's country, or one's religion, rather than love of All That Is.

War on anyone or anything alienates others, creating greater separation between 'us' and 'them'. To bring more peace to the world, start seeing every being as one of 'us', and sharing your love with 'them' as well as 'us'.

To bring more peace to the world, avoid violence, including in movies. You cannot bring about world peace while you continue to promote violence, inflict violence, and watch violence. Many elected officials are supported by industries which support violence. Don't vote for violence.

You are one with all of life, and all life is precious. Veganism helps remove violence from the world. A vegan diet helps with your health, the animals' health, and allows the animals to emit balancing positive energy, moving the planet towards the New Spirituality. Prayers of gratitude for the plants' and animals' sacrifice of their fruit and their lives helps.

Try making important decisions during meditation or when first awaking, when the ego voice is quiet. You may find decision making easier after 'sleeping on it'. It is best to consider the consequences of your thoughts and actions for All That Is and pray for help. You can ask that all decisions be based on the good of All That Is—based on love. Asking "What would serve All That Is at this time?" is the same as asking "What would love do now?"

A recipe for a loving world is to a) talk about love, b) love yourself, and c) open your heart by first forgiving those who have hurt you and allowing yourself to love all you meet.

Love and faith create miracles.

When faced with fear, think love, and ask: "What would love do now?" Take love with you wherever you go and you are invincible.

Teach your children that there is nothing to fear in this world or the next, and that they have angels and spirit guides on whom they can call to protect them.

Be who you are: love, peace, joy, and freedom. Be love, speak love, and act with love.

Everything of the light is one. You are the light of the world. Remember that everyone is equally capable of brilliance.

Each person has a divine mission aimed at bringing more love to the world. To do that, you need to step out of your comfort zone to step up and speak out about love. There may be past hurts you need to let go of and people you need to forgive before you are ready to step into your role. You may need to shine light on your shadows and release your stored emotions.

Do not fear your shadows. With love, they become extensions of the light. Express your natural emotions, rather than suppressing them. Counting to ten when you are angry gives you time to consider how you want to express your anger. Base your choices on love, not fear.

Surround yourself in white light energy and clear your energy field regularly. Your angels can help with this, with releasing unloving behaviours, and with residing in the present moment.

God has provided you with an internal guidance system which will lead you to joy. Your internal guidance system is the voice of your soul, that part of you closest to God. You can hear the voice of your higher self and spiritual helpers by meditating regularly and following your feelings. Follow your feelings towards joy, and away from discomfort. In the New Spirituality, life will be more joyful because people will be listening to their higher selves.

Your ego hijacks your communication between your higher self and your body with fear.

People don't need to be faultless to be loved, including you. What you see as flaws in yourselves are merely opportunities for growth. Your ego is helping you become the person your soul desires you to be, by providing you with opportunities to practise falling down and getting back up, stronger than before.

Your ego erects barricades that stop your heart from emitting peace. You remove those barricades by putting your soul in charge. You do that by thinking love before all you think, say and do, by meditating regularly, and by listening to your feelings, which are the voice of your soul.

Physical love on this planet is fraught with difficulties, which can be overcome once we learn to love ourselves emotionally first. Once you have learned to love yourself, it is easier to share your love with others. Talking about all forms of love and sex will help.

Sex can be a means to get close to God. Learn to love yourself emotionally, and then physically. Communication is key to achieving joyful loving sex. Talk about sex at every opportunity, with your partner and with friends.

When you think love, be love, and act with love, anything is possible, including helping to bring about the new Golden Age of love. You can help bring about this new age more quickly by communicating with your angels regularly, by meditating often, by thinking love as much as possible, by living in the present moment, and by sharing your love with all you meet. You can also send love out into the world and it is returned tenfold. You can use lovemaking sex to create more love to send out into the world, and have it returned tenfold.

Follow Jesus' example and think love before all that you do. Jesus provided examples for us all, but each of us is an example for someone as we all learn to become unconditionally loving to all. Each of us has a role to play in bringing about the new world. Each of us has been given a way to shine our light into the world.

In the New Spirituality, you can have a closer relationship with God, with your angels, your spirit guides, the Ascended Masters, and your ancestors. In the New Spirituality, everyone will think love before everything they think, say, and do. In the New Spirituality, it will be a joy to be of service to others. Telepathic communication with animals and other humans will make it easier to do that well. Highly Evolved Beings from other planets are waiting for more love to be evident on our planet before coming to teach us how to supercharge our love.

If you desire lessons in thinking love in difficult circumstances, ask and you shall receive.

You can spread the word about the miraculous power of love.

There is only one absolute truth and that is love. When you allow love to rule your life, you are always acting from the source of absolute truth. Love means allowing others the freedom to act from that same source in whatever way it presents itself to them.

Your soul will lead you to God. Your ego will try to lead you away from God and towards fear. God can allow you to feel some of her love—the honey-pot of ecstasy.

The God of Ultimate Reality is unchanging, unconditional love. The God of time and space is all things. Life is what God is, and God is in all of God's creation. All of life is love.

God's preferred name is Love, but as everything is made of love, God suggests you call her/him by the name which makes you think of love when you hear it.

In Ultimate Reality, God is only conscious of love. Consciousness is where God and its separate beings meet. Consciousness is what makes us one.

You are a spiritual child of God, created in the spiritual image of God, not the physical image of God. God cannot impel you to act as God, because free will is paramount. God gave you angels to help you act as God. You are here to learn about life, love, God, and about yourself.

Thoughts of love towards a virus and those affected by it can help eradicate the imbalance which causes a pandemic, rather than aiming to eradicate the virus with thoughts of war on the virus. Letting go of fear of COVID and honouring your body with healthy food and lifestyle improves your immunity.

Have faith in yourself and your creator. You can call on your spiritual helpers for help. Archangel Michael can help increase your confidence and faith and help keep you safe and healthy.

In order to see the planet become more pristine, take personal responsibility and give this a higher priority in your life. Keep in touch with Mother Earth (literally), allowing you to feel her love, and moving her up your priority list. You can send your peace, love, healing, and joy out into the world—to all the people and creatures of the Earth, and to Mother Earth herself.

Consider the consequences of all your actions and non-actions to the planet and your future. For instance, you can:

- Vote for a government which considers the planet.
- Buy from suppliers which consider the planet.
- Speak out about the need to consider the planet.
- Use electric cars.
- Install solar panels.
- Pick up rubbish.
- Sign petitions.
- Write letters to members of Parliament and suppliers.

When your physical body dies, you just change form—back to Earth, God-mind, and spirit.

Expressing love allows you to experience love. When you

start to follow your feelings, you realise that what might be appropriate in one moment may not be appropriate in the next. If you think love before taking any action, all will be well.

Lessons about reducing suffering in life:

- Think love before all that you do.
- Live in the moment.
- Follow your feelings towards joy and away from discomfort.

Meditation helps release stress. There are other ways of reducing stress which all bring you back to the present moment, where there is nothing to stress about. God resides in the present moment, and it is where you find joy.

The ego creates conflict to separate you from God and everybody else. Any conflict between you and another is a reflection of the conflict in your mind. To keep itself separate, the ego creates someone who is the 'other'. Understanding the reason for the conflict is the key to ending it. Love doesn't need to be right. Someone 'pressing your buttons' makes your ego feel attacked. Your higher self can take charge by first loving your ego, and then sending love to the 'other'.

God could not intervene in the treatment of the Jews by the Nazis, as free will is paramount. All those souls whose physical lives ended at the hands of the Nazis incarnated knowing this would be the way they would leave their physical lives. Even though both instigators and victims were acting as 'friendly souls' allowing the other to learn spiritual lessons, there are still consequences, known to some as karma. If one asks: "What would love do now?" chances are the answer would be to forgive all those who cause suffering. First love yourself in relation to the Holocaust, and then send love to those involved, and all generations since.

Love can end conflict in Israel/Palestine and throughout the Middle East. "Thank you, God for providing a peaceful solution to the conflict in Palestine/Israel and throughout the Middle East." Grievances and suffering need to be acknowledged and forgiven. Layers of pain have accumulated in the Middle East and other countries where conflict has ensued. Each layer needs to be acknowledged, peeled back, and love and forgiveness applied to each layer.

Authority figures' guidance and peer pressure can override your internal guidance systems, allowing you to carry out evil acts against others in order not to be included in the 'others'. Everyone is capable of evil acts, once they create any other being as the 'other'. The best way to have a positive outcome is to think love before all that you think, say, and do, and to listen to your feelings, which are the voice of your soul. Follow Jesus' example to love your neighbour as yourself, and to stand up against others who want to cast the first stone.

The best way to see more love in the world is to lead by example:

- Give love to others.
- Send your love out into the world.

- Think love before all that you do.
- Smile at others.
- Compliment and appreciate others.
- Offer hugs, kisses, and small acts of kindness.
- Help others.
- Give small gifts.
- Share your love in your individual role.

Make love the dominant force in your life by thinking love before all that you think, say, and do, and by asking: "What would love do now?" when faced with a decision.

❈❈❈

Sometimes the more we learn about a subject, the more questions arise and that has been my experience with this book. Rather than asking any more of my questions and relating those answers to you, I encourage you to have your own conversations with God and your angels. I would love to hear what questions arose for you and any answers you received. Sometimes the questions are just as enlightening as the answers.

You can contact me by email at lorelle@lorelletaylor.com or on my Facebook page www.facebook.com/LorelleKTaylor or connect with me on my Instagram page @lorelle_taylor

For further information received from spiritual beings and God, see my blog at https://www.lorelletaylor.com

You can find out how I learned to communicate with spiritual beings and God by reading my first book: *Getting*

Used to Weird: A Very Different Sort of Love Story. My second book, *WE ARE ONE*, contains further lessons, and answers questions to God about the major religions.

Acknowledgements

As most of this book was channelled information, the writing of it was relatively easy compared to my earlier books. The editing of it was another matter entirely. I am so grateful to my editor Lauren Elise Daniels. Not only did she provide a great edit, she inspired me to look at the work with a critical eye as well.

I would like to thank Ronald from cruzialdesigns at 99designs for a brilliant cover, both in the literal and figurative sense.

I will also take this opportunity to thank God and the angels for the words on the page, and the joy and love they shared.

I would also like to thank you, the reader. Thank you for helping me to create the world of my dreams, where love rules, peace reigns, and everyone is treated with respect.

Bibliography

[1] GETTING USED TO WEIRD: A Very Different Sort of Love Story, Lorelle Taylor. Peace Angel, Brisbane, 2019.

[2] WE ARE ONE, Lorelle Taylor. Peace Angel, Brisbane, 2020

[3] BILLIE DEAN'S 30 DAYS OF WYLD SHAMANISM COURSE (Previously 30 days of Spiritual Wildness) https://billiedean.com/ (for the Deep Peace Trust https://deeppeacetrust.com/)

[4] TOMORROW'S GOD: Our Greatest Spiritual Challenge, Neale Donald Walsch. Atria, New York, 2004.

[5] MAKING LOVE TO GOD: The Path to Divine Sex, Ananda through Tina Louise Spalding. Light Technology, Flagstaff AZ, 2013.

[6] A FIVE STEP PLAN TO FEED THE WORLD https://www.nationalgeographic.com/foodfeatures/feeding-9-billion/

[7] ASK YOUR ANGELS, Alma Daniel, Timothy Wyllie, and Andrew Ramer. Ballantine, New York, 1992.

[8] THE SHADOW EFFECT ONLINE COURSE, Debbie Ford https://www.hayhouse.com/the-shadow-effect-debbie-ford-online-course

[9] THE JOY OF JESUS, Doreen Virtue, 2018.

[10] THE JOY OF JESUS, Doreen Virtue, 2018.

[11] A COURSE IN MIRACLES, scribed by Helen Schucman. Foundation for Inner Peace, Mill Valley, CA, 2007.

[12] A COURSE IN MIRACLES, scribed by Helen Schucman. Foundation for Inner Peace, Mill Valley, CA, 2007.

[13] BECOMING ENLIGHTENED, His Holiness the Dalai Lama, (Jeffrey Hopkins, Trans. & Ed.). Ebury, London, 2010.

[14] GETTING USED TO WEIRD: A Very Different Sort of Love Story, Lorelle Taylor. Peace Angel, Brisbane, 2019.

[15] THE FEMALE ARCHANGELS: Reclaim Your Power with the Lost Teachings of the Divine Feminine, Claire Stone. Hay House, Carlsbad CA, 2020.

[16] TOMORROW'S GOD: Our Greatest Spiritual Challenge, Neale Donald Walsch. Atria, New York, 2004.

[17] TOMORROW'S GOD: Our Greatest Spiritual Challenge, Neale Donald Walsch. Atria, New York, 2004.

[18] THE LUCIFER EFFECT: How Good People Turn Evil, Philip Zimbardo. Rider, New York, 2007.

[19] CONFORMITY WAITING ROOM EXPERIMENT
https://www.youtube.com/watch?v=X6kWygqR0L8

[20] THE LUCIFER EFFECT: How Good People Turn Evil, Philip Zimbardo. Rider, New York, 2007.

[21] WE ARE ONE, Lorelle Taylor. Peace Angel, Brisbane, 2020

www.ingramcontent.com/pod-product-compliance
Lightning Source LLC
Chambersburg PA
CBHW030253010526
44107CB00053B/1687